# FIRST BYTE

choosing and using a home computer

# FIRST BYTE

## choosing and using a home computer

MIKE SCOTT ROHAN

EP Publishing Limited

For my parents



ISBN 0 7158 0866 4 (casebound)
ISBN 0 7158 0867 2 (paperback)

**British Library Cataloguing in Publication Data**
Rohan, Michael Scott
First byte.
1. Microcomputers—Amateur's manuals
I. Title
001.64' 04 OA76.5
ISBN 0-7158-0867-2

First edition 1983

Published by EP Publishing Limited, Bradford Road, East Ardsley, Wakefield, West Yorkshire, WF3 2JN, England

Published in Australia by
Australia and New Zealand Book Co. Pty. Ltd., 10 Aquatic Drive, Frenchs Forest, N.S.W. 2086

ISBN 0 85552 130 9

Typeset by Letaseta, Otley, West Yorkshire, England

Colour reproduction by Colthouse Repro Ltd., Bournemouth, Dorset, England.

Printed and bound in Italy by
Legatoria Editoriale Giovanni Olivotto, Vicenza

Cartoons by Jim Barker

Other illustrations by Douglas Hewitt

Design by Krystyna Hewitt

Cover computercake made by Deborah Rohan

# Contents

A computer in your home—once a science-fiction writer's dream, now an adman's. But what will it really mean to **you**?

# Acknowledgements

I would like to thank everyone who has helped in the creation of this book, but most of all Philip Gardner of EP Publishing, for vigorous organisation and support; Dermot Dobson, technical wizard, for supervising photography; Jim Barker, for the alternative view; Maggie Noach, agent extraordinary; and, as ever, my wife Deb, for unflagging backup, superhuman patience, and cake icing everywhere. Also thanks to Krystyna, Doug and Oliver Hewitt, and to the many manufacturers and loyal PR men who have assisted us, in particular Atari (UK) Ltd and Barry Millns of Burson-Marsteller Ltd, and to Micropower Ltd of Leeds.
We are also grateful for the assistance of several software publishers who supplied interesting material; regrettably, there was not room to make direct use of all of it. Finally, to ICL, who got me into this in the first place.

**Photograph credits**

Acornsoft Ltd: 6, 19 (bottom), 27, 51, 74, 79
Apple Computer (UK) Ltd: 47
Atari (UK) Ltd: 10 (top), 22, 48, 62
Camputers Ltd: 64 (top)
Commodore Business Machines (UK) Ltd: 52, 57, 68
Dean Electronics Ltd: 44
Dermot Dobson 14, 15, 17 (top), 18, 19 (top), 33, 34, 46, 66, 75, 83
EP Publishing Ltd/Philip Gardner: 16 (right), 20, 39, 40, 43, 58, 63 (top), 67
Grundy Business Systems Ltd: 65
Jupiter Cantab Ltd: 56 (top)
Lowe Electronics Ltd: 54, 60 (top)
Memotech Ltd: 38, 56 (bottom)
Microwriter Ltd: 49
Oric Products International Ltd: 6, 55, 59 (top)
Sharp Electronics (UK) Ltd: 69
Sinclair Research Ltd: 10 (bottom), 16 (left), 17 (bottom), 59 (bottom)
Sord Computer Systems Inc: 11, 60 (bottom)
Tandy Corporation Ltd: 63 (bottom)
Texas Instruments Ltd: 61
John Williams Studio Ltd: cover, 3

# 1. What's this all about?

What indeed—something new and exciting that's going to make dramatic changes in all our lives, or just a neat little electronic calculating device small enough to sit in the living-room, plugged into the family TV? The answer is both. Computers are the most revolutionary arrival in the home since television or radio or the gramophone; they are likely to affect our lives more than all of those put together, and probably for the better. Computers aren't just passive entertainment you sit and gawp at; they involve you. **They talk back.**

**First Byte** isn't a complete guide to everything about home computers, because no book could be. You should treat any such claims with deep suspicion. The fact is that the whole field is so large, and changing so fast, that there are only two ways to explore it. One is by following some, at least, of the many magazines now catering for the home-computer user; the other, more important, way is by having and using your own home computer.

There's just one drawback. To do either of these things properly you need to have at least some basic grasp of the subject. You can pick it up in time, of course, but that can be a painful, discouraging and often very expensive process. Some magazines honestly try to cater for newcomers, but they can't devote much space to it—understandably; they rely on a **continuing** readership, month after month. Beginners don't stay beginners long in computing—it's too much fun, and just difficult enough to make you feel you're accomplishing something—so if they kept on repeating elementary material they'd soon lose sales. And you certainly need to know something about home computers before you set out to buy one; they aren't all alike, they won't all do the same things, and they vary enormously in price. You could make some really expensive blunders very easily. This is where **First Byte** comes in.

I wanted to write a book of this kind because I could have used one myself when I was just beginning to get interested in home computers, some years ago. Then as now it seemed to me that too many 'introductory' books were written **by** computer freaks **for** ready-made computer freaks—very technically-minded people, like radio hams or motorcycle worshippers, who quickly fall in love with the sheer intricacies of a subject for its own sake. They live, breathe and talk little else—fine for them, but both boring and off-putting to the rest of us. Some of them actually seem to resent making things easier for newcomers, as if that somehow cheapened the subject. That is a terrible shame, because it simply isn't true. Less dedicated people can still get a great deal out of home computers, and more productively, because they actually **use** the machines for something and not as an end in themselves: they enhance their lives with them. And that is where the real future of home computers lies—not with the sheer fanatics.

This book, then, is an introduction for ordinary people who might be put off by a barrage of jargon and technicalities. Of course, **some** jargon is necessary; computers have introduced new concepts into our lives, so new words are needed to describe them. But it should never be the barrier it sometimes becomes. Equally, some technicalities are necessary—eventually. But if you have some idea, even a general one, of the actual processes that lie behind them, you will find that you can pick up more exact knowledge as you go along; the details fall quite naturally into place. The important thing is not to discourage you, but to get you off to a good start, and that is what I have set out to do.

**First Byte** is an introduction, and so meant to be outgrown—the sooner the better. Because of this we

Office, school and home—the three worlds of the microcomputer

have done our best to keep the price reasonable—cartoons by Jim Barker, well known to science-fiction fans all over the world, are our only luxury, and we have not tied ourselves to manufacturers or dealers by carrying advertising. We simply offer you some idea of what home computers can do for you (and what they will soon be able to do); of how they work (and how they were made to work); of the other equipment you may need to get the best out of them; of how to make them do what **you** want; and of which ones you can go out and buy.

After that, it's really over to you. All we can do is point you in the right direction, with a few helpful hints and a short glossary of common jargon we haven't covered elsewhere. But by far the best piece of advice we can give you is never to be put off by the mysticism that surrounds computers at so many levels. They can be complicated—sometimes—but they are rarely as forbidding as they look at first; if you make the effort, you will soon find yourself coping almost automatically with something that once looked baffling. And in the years to come they are likely to get easier, not harder to use, as they become less and less the concern of the computer profession and are used by people who can't spare the time to acquire vastly detailed skills. In the last few years some enlightened computer professionals have put immense efforts into crusades to make more people 'computer-literate', but recently one of them changed his mind, and decided to stress making computers more 'people-literate'—an immensely sensible decision, as technological advances make this more and more possible. But already home computers are probably easier to use than the family car, all things considered. They may even be more fun.

When you have finished **First Byte** there will be many magazines to help you, and other computer books to buy. Most of all, though, there will be an extraordinary little device to entertain, extend and occasionally infuriate you. Don't give up. Stick to it; make friends with it. It's worth it—wait and see.

### So what is a home computer?

A computer—any computer—is a device which can receive and understand information, process that information according to instructions, and produce appropriate results. The physical parts of a computer—'the bits,' as one early pioneer put it, 'you can kick!'—are generally known as the **hardware**; by the warped mental processes of computer experts, therefore, the information the hardware handles has become known as **software.**

The three main types of computer—mainframe, mini and micro

These are really the only two pieces of computer jargon you need remember for the moment.

In the beginning computers were only those giant faceless machines we know and loathe from films, endless rows of steel wardrobes that click and whirr and flash meaningless little lights the whole length and breadth of an enormous vault-like room, with white-coated humans scurrying about ant-like to serve them. Occasionally, in between reducing your bank balance by a factor of ten and sending you the known universe's gas bill, they took over the world.

Such computers are still around, though it's mostly their supporting devices that take up the space, and they rarely, if ever, misbehave; only humans can do that. But technological advances have crammed much more 'thinking' capacity into the same space—so much more that it became possible to build smaller and cheaper computers that had as much power as the original giant 'mainframe'. These little fellows—ranging from the size of an average office to that of a desk—became known as **minicomputers.** But in time the development of microchip technology, of which more later, crammed **so** much more capacity into them that even smaller computers could be built, able now to sit on top of a desk; these were called **microcomputers.**

But meanwhile wicked and time-wasting computer workers and students had discovered that you could work out your income tax or play crazy games on computers, and they began buying the smaller microcomputers to carry on doing this at home. One of them harnessed a simple computer to play one game—**Pong**, a kind of electronic table-tennis—when you put a coin in a slot, and invented the video games now so common in pubs, clubs and amusement arcades. Meanwhile many businessmen were finding it quicker and simpler to learn to use these microcomputers themselves, rather than have the giant 'macrocomputer' in the cellar chew their work over when it eventually finished recalculating the company payroll and playing chess with the support staff. They too began to take their interests home.

And so a number of manufacturers began to realise that there was a market for microcomputers that were neither wholly business-oriented nor just entertainment boxes, like so-called TV games—machines that could put the power and flexibility of a real computer, as powerful as the original macrocomputers once were, into the hands of ordinary people, and so vastly enrich their lives. How? Read on, and see.

# 2. What would I do with a home computer?

The shortest answer to that is—work, and play. In the computer man has invented the greatest aid to both these activities since the wheel. The sheer range of things you can do with a home computer is enormous—some useful, some entertaining, all interesting. In a chapter like this we can only skim the surface, looking at some of the commonest uses. But I hope, frankly, that this will be enough to hook you, until you are sufficiently at home with computers to let your own experience and imagination take over—as they undoubtedly will. You will find uses for your computer that nobody else can, because, at its best, it becomes that most valuable thing—an extension of yourself.

Contrary to popular opinion, you don't need to be some kind of scientific superbrain to use a computer like that. You can do most of the things we look at here without ever understanding how the computer works, and many without even learning how to give it its instructions—'program' it—yourself. Packaged programs are available for almost everything, and all you generally need to know is how to load them in—not difficult! Then just follow the instructions. But that is a little like owning a plane and just taxiing it around the runway. Learning to program, like anything worthwhile, does take a little effort; some people find it easy, others—like me—less so. But all you really need is a little patience, and less maths than one O-level paper; you can see for yourself in chapter 6. You can get by without programming, but you will miss the immense satisfaction of bringing the computer's power to bear on an idea or a problem of your own—of reducing a tedious or difficult task, such as keeping club records, to a simple routine the computer handles with minimum interference from you. A warm glow comes back every time you think 'But I used to spend an **evening** doing this!' There is only one danger—you may spend the time you save playing, or even devising, computer games instead.

In an ideal world work and play would be much the same things, combining the benefit of one with the pleasure of the other. Computers may be beginning to blur the distinction, but it still exists. Home computers will handle many business-related functions, but they also have to handle games and hobby functions; the two demand rather different resources and capabilities, and it is hard to provide both equally in one inexpensive machine. Naturally the bias is towards the pleasure side in most home machines. But more straight-faced users need not despair; the capacities of all but the smallest home machines exceed those of machines that were sold for small-business use only a few years ago, and they are far cheaper. A home machine can make a good starting point for the small businessman anxious to learn something about computers before making a heavy capital investment, and he may be surprised at just how much they can actually cope with. Even the sober business user, though, often succumbs to the insidious lure of games, so with them we will start.

## Games

A computer is like a chess set that fights back. Its ability to respond 'intelligently' makes it a very stimulating adversary or partner, and it has the unique ability to set the scene for you—anything from chessboard or bridge tables to battlefields or the depths of space, anywhere the imagination can reach. The huge variety of games you can play on a

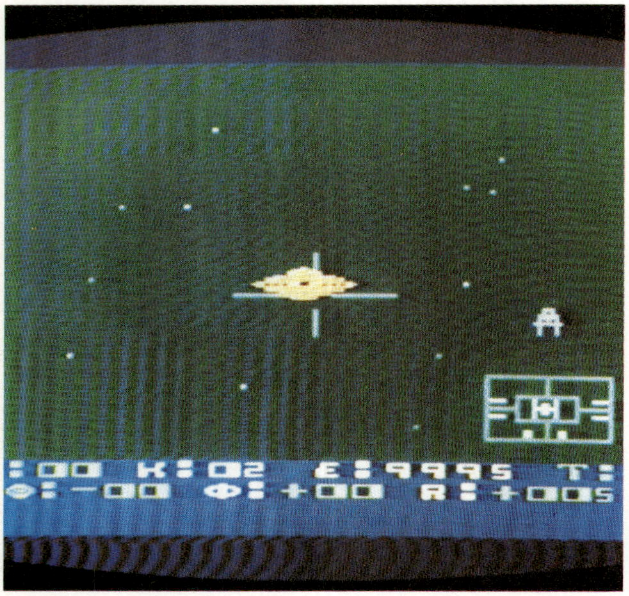

Atari's **Star Raiders,** voted Game of the Year in a recent magazine poll, puts you vividly at the controls of a spacecraft, fighting dogfight duels with enemy craft to defend starbases such as this. But you must also keep track of your position, power levels and damage suffered—shown on the 'instrument panel' at the bottom of the screen

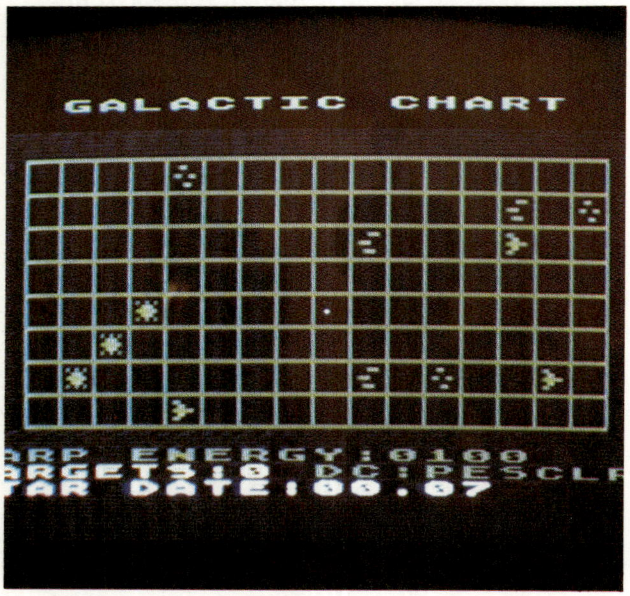


You can refit your craft at starbases, but it takes strategy to decide just when, and skill to navigate your craft between zones on the constantly-changing galactic chart, and to dock it when you reach the base. Meanwhile, the enemy is re-grouping...

home computer falls broadly into two categories—those that actually depict what is happening, and those that describe it.

**Arcade games**

The first kind are often known as 'arcade' games, because many of them are ones you will recognise from those pinging and bleeping machines in pubs, clubs, cafés, and of course amusement arcades—**Space Invaders** and its many descendants. All the favourites are available, in some form, for just about every computer in this book—**Invaders, Galaxians, PacMan, Missile Command, Frogger, Defender** and many more. But such games have to be designed to break down neatly into a coin's worth of time, a limitation unnecessary on the computer. Many arcade-style games, such as Atari's excellent **Star Raiders,** can therefore be made much more complex and involving, to the point where they demand real strategic skill and judgement. Computer simulations

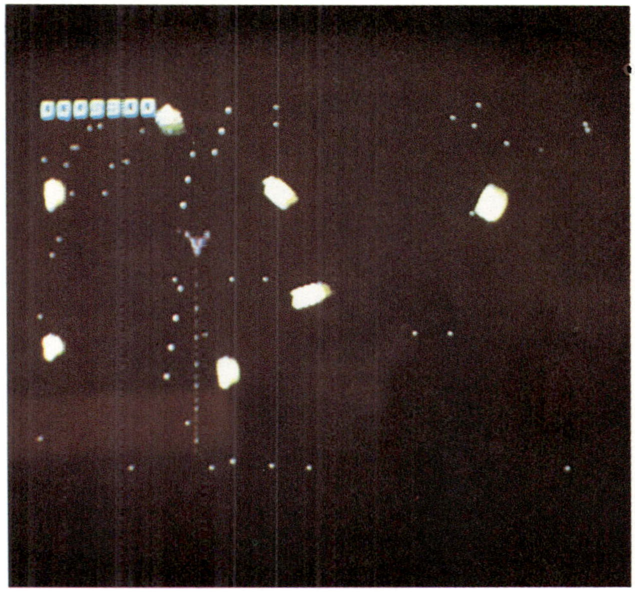

Even less expensive machines can produce impressive games, like Psion Software's **Asteroids**-style game **Planetoids** for the minimum-memory version of the Spectrum

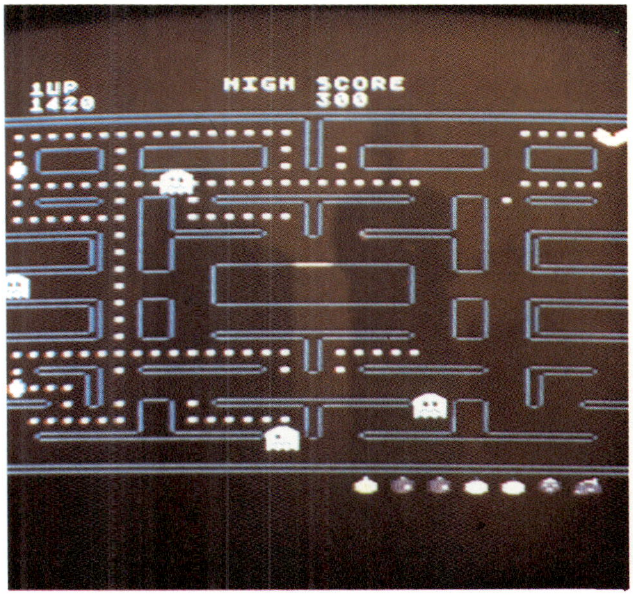


The arcade-machine favourite **Pacman** has appeared in some form or other for just about every home computer—this is Atari's authorized version

of popular sports such as soccer and basketball are also available—with animated players you control, and suitably cheering crowds—as well as less likely ones such as skiing, golf, and even darts. Some arcade-style simulations practically escape from the definition of 'game'. Flight-simulation programs are available which reproduce the control panel and windscreen of a plane; you 'fly' it with the computer's controls. Some of the better ones are so realistic they are often used for preliminary pilot training in the USA, and highly authentic versions are available for even the smallest computers on the market. It appears there is even a simulator for the Space Shuttle!

Of course, if all you want is the commoner arcade games, and not detailed simulations such as these, you will also find them on so-called TV games machines. Actually, a TV game is nothing but a half-baked computer. The pictures it produces—in computer parlance its 'graphics'—may in the best models be a little better than the average general-purpose computer, but the variety of games it can play is far lower, and the cost of them far higher. TV games programs usually come in cartridges; these are expensive, because they contain electronic components known as ROM chips. Many computers can also load in programs this way, but all of them more commonly use plain audio cassettes and cassette recorders—slower but much cheaper—or magnetic disks, more efficient than either and in the long run cheaper than cartridges. All the programs, the 'software', that we look at in this chapter are sold in one of these forms.

Almost every common board game—chess, backgammon, draughts, Scrabble—and card game—poker, blackjack, bridge—can be played on, and with, a home computer, and it is with games like this that they score especially well over TV games machines. The computer's greater memory and 'reasoning' power lets it play all these games at a much higher and more realistic level. Chess programs vary enormously, but a good one will give you a clear display of board and pieces—in colour, if the machine has that facility—and will be able to play at a number of different skill levels. Many can also time moves, record them, replay the game and record it onto cassette—very useful if you have to leave off halfway through. Sophisticated ones will even play specified gambits, set and solve problems or analyse games; for one quite cheap computer there is even one which talks, telling you its move and adding sharp comments on yours... Card games are also commonly available; with a computer you need never be stuck for a fourth, or even all the other players! Casino games such as chemin-de-fer or roulette can be played just as easily, the computer providing cards or wheel and table. But beware—your friends will want to try it, and when they get skinned they may not believe it isn't you pulling the electronic strings! Or your computer could even end up owning **you**...

You can set a good chess program to various levels of skill—but never underestimate it!

**Text-based games**

The second type of game doesn't sound quite so exciting—no pretty pictures, nothing but text, with a few diagrams at best. But if you try one you may be surprised. It is very much like the difference between a film and a book; one faces you with someone else's imagination, the other stimulates yours. A text-based game is like a book that fights back. And it has many other advantages, not least that by using so few graphics it leaves much of the computer's memory free for sheer detail. The earliest computer games, played in spare moments on giant macro systems by their support staff, were text games, and at least one, based loosely on the TV series **Star Trek**, is still common; another favourite is derived from the cult game **Dungeons & Dragons.** It comes under many titles, **Adventure** being one of the commonest. These games describe your progress through a complicated setting—outer space, or sinister labyrinths haunted by trolls, sorcerers and similar fantastic creatures—feeding you information and getting you into situations you have to work your way out of. The computer acts as your starship's crew and computers, obeying

Text games may **look** less exciting than their arcade cousins, but you never know just what'll be lurking behind that North exit—especially if you forget to read the sign...

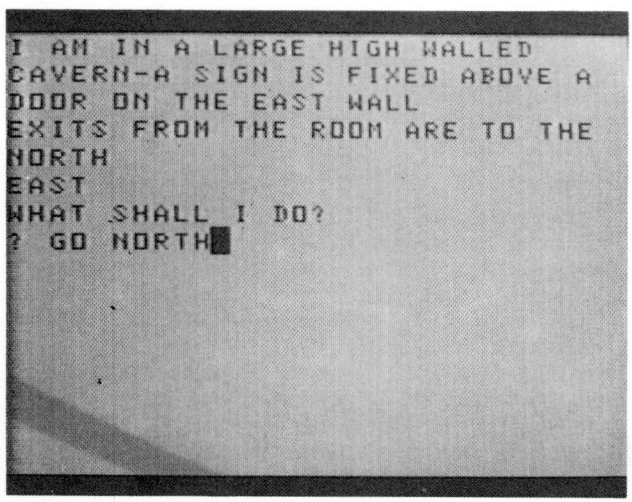

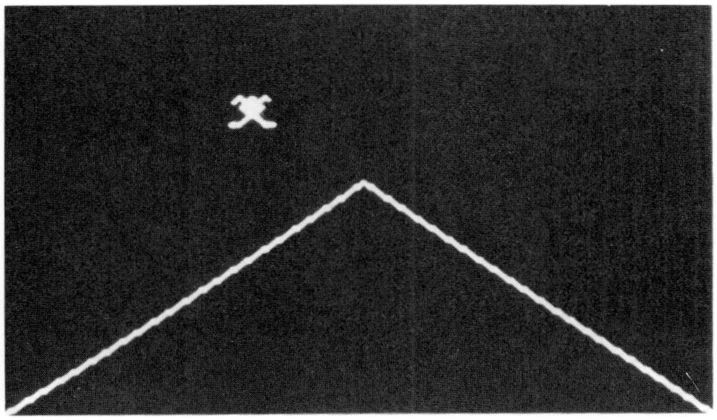

A simple arcade-style shooting game—but it was devised by writer Allan Scott after only a few **hours**' first-time experience on a home computer

your orders and reporting the situation to you, or as your guide and counsellor in this fantasy world. But if your imagination doesn't work that way, you can always rule an authentic medieval kingdom, balancing your military and economic policies against bad harvests, unruly nobles and suitably revolting peasants. If you've ever wanted to run a hotel, an airline or a car company, or to be Prime Minister, there are programs to put you in the hot seat. In text games you can fight the great battles of the Civil or Napoleonic Wars, or the whole of World War II (from either side). The format has even been adapted to soft-core sex escapades. But personally I'm inclined to resist automation in **that** department, at least.

Passing hurriedly on, it may be that other people's games don't appeal, or that you get tired of playing the ones that do, and feel you could do better yourself. Well, why not try? One novice I know was starting his first game after only an hour or two with his machine—nothing very complex, of course, but he was able to improve it step by step as his knowledge increased. On one or two machines the manufacturers go out of their way to help games designers by providing so-called sprite graphics, picture elements that can be moved smoothly and easily around the screen, in shapes and colours you define—as Space Invaders and missiles, for example. To write really good games, though, you are going to have to master all aspects of programming pretty thoroughly. But that, as I hope you will find out, can be great fun.

## Education

If I've spent so much time on games, it is because that is what first attracts many people, especially young people, to home computers. But these extraordinary machines can do a great deal more than just entertain, valuable as this is. They have enormous potential as an aid to education, in any number of ways.

The same methods they use to make games so

A computer puts life into this geography quiz, **and** prints out your results on paper

involving, their animated graphics and their ability to react and respond—their 'interactive' qualities—can be used to teach and communicate on quite a high level. Some educational programs are very like games; in one, based on the famous film **Fantastic Voyage**, the player follows a quest game through an animated map of the human body, fending off attacks by its immune system, and in the process learns quite a lot about anatomy and physiology. But most educational programs available are more straightforward teaching sessions in which the computer sets out information, illustrates it, and asks the pupil questions; if these aren't satisfactorily answered, the computer will work through the relevant part of the program again, sometimes with some extra explanation. In maths programs the problems come alive; animated diagrams in chemistry programs show the molecules of two substances reacting with each other to form other compounds, and in physics programs how airflow creates lift. Many home computers have sound and speech reproduction or even simulation facilities that can be used to teach foreign languages, illustrating the examples and pronouncing them correctly. Geography and history programs benefit from animated maps that can be directly tied in with facts and figures. Subjects for the more advanced student, such as economics and statistics, also benefit from being taught by computer, because these subjects are becoming increasingly computer-based. The same applies to electronics; it would be possible for a computer to 'model' the actions of components in a circuit diagram, so the student could draw his own and see at once whether it worked or not and why. I have not seen such a program, but if it isn't here yet, it's only a matter of time.

Educational programs are available for most of the computers in this book, and no doubt soon will be for the rest; Atari have probably the biggest range at present, but there are ambitious plans for the Sinclair range. But a cautionary note is called for—not all educational programs are good. Some are limited by the abilities of the particular computer, others by the limited imagination of their authors—much the worse handicap. Too much educational software for home machines works less well than an ordinary textbook, and costs more—a graveyard of lost opportunities. American-originated material is almost always well presented and worthwhile, but may be too limited and 'young' for its prescribed age range; US education tends to lag behind its European counterpart right up to graduate level. And it can also be irritatingly insular, as with one program that insisted World War II started in 1940! In assessing educational programs, look for one that involves the user rather than just lecturing him. Programs that are just question-and-answer quizzes are rarely much use. The best ones are usually written by qualified teachers to specific syllabuses such as GCE O-level, and have full supporting text

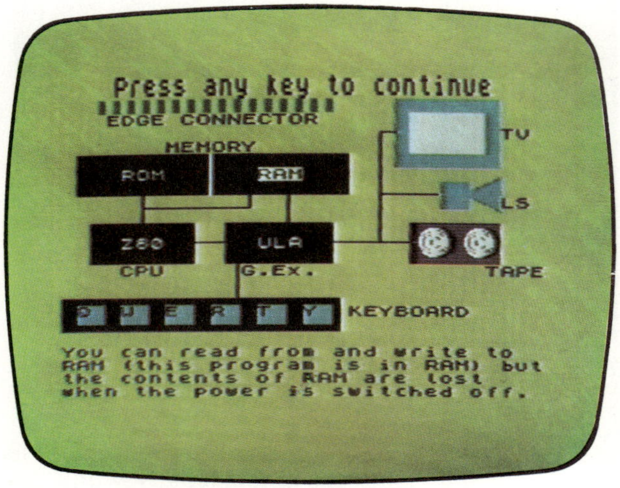


Having a computer is the best way to learn about computers—and it can teach you itself

material. But, as with everything else in this book, look before you buy!

**Computer education**

By having a computer you learn about computers. There really isn't a better way. Computer skill might not seem so important to the older generation, but every school now offers some form of computer instruction, and at many US universities nobody can take a degree in **any** subject—maths, physics, French, history, English literature—without passing a course in basic computer skills. There is a sound reason for this. Over the next decade or two computers are going to become the main way of storing and finding information about almost anything, and it will become increasingly difficult to follow any career more complex than digging ditches without running into them. The Department of Education has launched a scheme to make sure every school in Britain has at least one computer; of the machines approved under this scheme two—the BBC micro and the Sinclair Spectrum—are covered in this book. (The third, Research Machines' 480Z, is excellent, but a little too expensive for most home users.) However, the amount of time a child can spend on a school machine will naturally be limited; unlimited time on his own home machine will help his studies. A computer isn't any kind of short cut to thought; he/she will learn more about maths and logic through programming than with a pocket calculator. And if he/she really takes to computing, it can turn to advantage; the Extended BASIC language for the Commodore 64 computer was developed by a 16-year-old British schoolboy. It is expected to bring him in really huge royalties. An extreme case—but computing, and especially smaller-scale computing, is one of the few areas where opportunities are presently increasing rather than shrinking. Even sending in a simple game to a

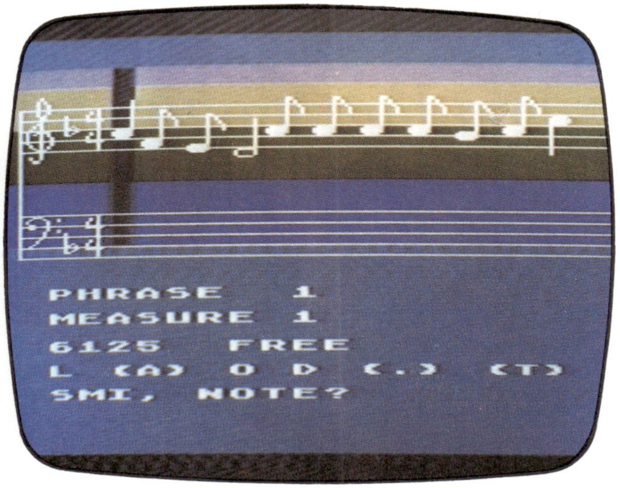


Learning music is much more fun with a program like this, which plays the notes as you enter them, stores them and repeats them as complete phrases or tunes you can edit, sing to or play along with

This attractive web shape is a simple three-dimensional graph; even more delicate and complicated forms can be made this way—the computer uniting mathematics and art

magazine can earn a few pounds, and selling more complex ones is becoming quite a lucrative cottage industry.

**Wider educational uses**
Education, of course, doesn't stop with purely academic subjects. Nor do the teaching abilities of a home computer. With decent sound facilities you can learn music notation, the 'printed' music on the screen interacting directly with the sound played, or even composition. Computer art is fun, but rarely reaches the same exalted level. A computer's display picture is built up of dots, not unlike a newspaper photograph but much coarser and in a very limited range of colours; relatively little shading is possible. The effect is cartoon-like, even on the best 'high-resolution' machines; however, the cartoons can be brought to life by animation—not the easiest of techniques, though there are special programs to help. The computer can also generate very beautiful abstract shapes on the screen by plotting graphs, even in three dimensions to create a 'wire-sculpture' effect. Its ability to generate 3-D diagrams can also be a valuable aid to design. However, graphics do eat up computer memory, especially in higher resolutions, where more dots must be generated.

For machines with proper typewriter-style keyboards you can nearly always buy programs to teach you touch-typing, a very valuable skill; they

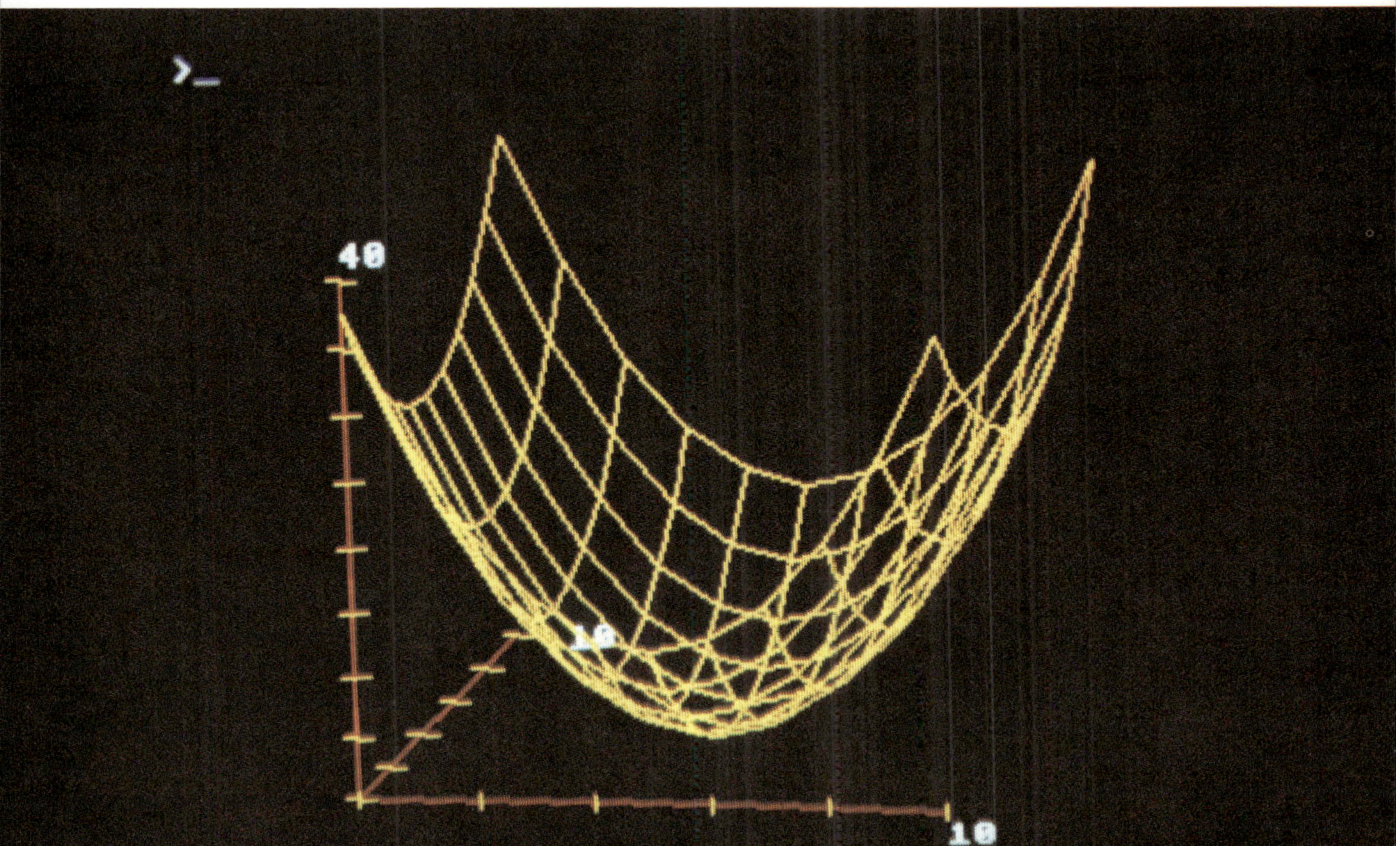

take you through several levels of skill, some of them to proper secretarial standard. With the arrival of speech facilities, shorthand dictation programs also become possible. Other possibilities include a sophisticated car-driving program, along the lines of the flight simulators we mentioned earlier—games for a serious purpose. Without actual controls its realism would be limited, but it could set up the kind of situation and problems the learner is likely to encounter—a skid, a confusing junction, a pedestrian stepping out from behind a parked car—and help inculcate that priceless quality, road sense. Programs such as this are bound to appear as computers get more sophisticated, and able to bring us closer and closer to real life. That, after all, is what education is all about.

## Business uses

As we will see, computers began life as purely mathematical and scientific devices, but by far their greatest role today—even including military uses—is as aids to commerce; most computers are business computers. Not only in giant multinationals, either; there may be one lurking in your doctor's or dental surgeon's surgery, or in the back room of the corner shop. It was the creation of small machines for small businesses that paved the way for the home computer; but, as I said earlier, their ways have tended to part more recently. Few of the smaller home machines retain much serious business potential, though they can do surprisingly well when pushed. But they are all more than up to taking care of those especially boring bits of business that filter into our everyday lives, in just the same way as a mighty macrocomputer runs a nationalised industry—or, on second thoughts, quite a bit better.

When you're in the red you know it, with this personal finances program

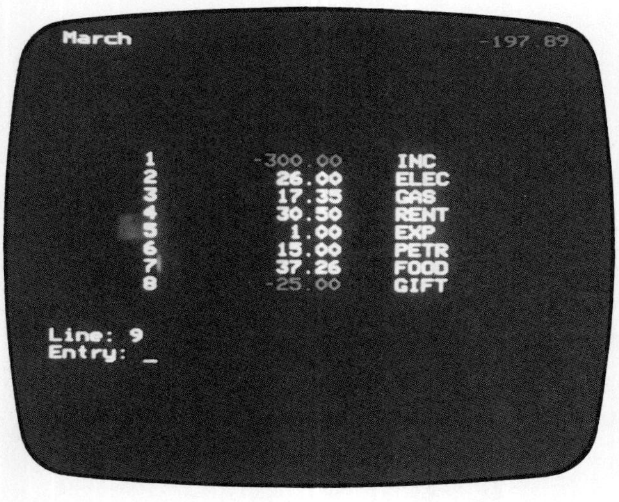


### Finances

Everybody's got 'em—rent, rates, mortgage, gas bill, phone bill, electricity bill, groceries, dog food, TV license, petrol... Sorry if I'm depressing you. A home computer won't make these things go away, but with the aid of a standard home-finance program, available for most computers, you can at least introduce some system and forward planning into the flow of cash in and out of your household. You enter all your transactions—income, regular payments in and out, cheques written, credit-card purchases and so on—into the computer; it records these in labelled areas of its memory called 'files'—for obvious reasons—and adds them to or deducts them from the appropriate accounts. It does all the calculation for you—mortgage and credit-card interest, how much you must save per month in the building society to reach a target. It can look ahead to remind you of payments due before your next expected income—you needn't be caught out by the half-yearly rates ever again.

Admittedly you need to be faithful and fairly systematic about filling things in—the computer can't chase you for them, after all—and it is unsystematic people who need such things most. But they may take to it because it reduces the hassle and confusion and the chances of making disappointing mistakes. And programs like these are a very good way for young people just beginning to manage their own money to develop the right kind of survival skills.

Tax is just about the biggest financial thorn in anyone's flesh, and the computer can help you here too; tax-handling programs are available for most home machines, even the smallest, and by asking you the right questions and doing the right calculations they can act as anchorman in your annual tug-o'-war with the Inland Revenue. But make sure you're working with up-to-date rates!

Again, make sure what you buy is written for your home market. There are a number of unreformed American programs on sale; this doesn't matter so much for home budgets, as the currencies are compatible and problems much the same anywhere, but they tend to have headings like ALIMONY and PSYCHIATRIST, the mere presence of which will cause your nearest and dearest to look upon you with suspicion. American tax programs, on the other hand, are almost always useless outside the U.S.—but some people still sell them.

### Small administrative tasks

If you're the kind of person who gets saddled with running every little organisation in sight, whether it's the Women's Institute, the Sea Scouts or the Neasden Liberation Front, a home computer is going to make your life easier. Societies, clubs, crèches even, all seem to need vast records kept, accounts rendered, rosters organised and mailings sent out. Buy a home computer—or, better still, talk the society into buying you one. With the aid of a fairly straightforward program known as a database, which functions like a kind of electronic filing cabinet, you can store records on ordinary audio cassettes (or disks, when you get very sophisticated); the computer can search through the 'files' to find the information you need, whether it's the ex-Treasurer's address in Rio, a list of people who **still** haven't paid for the last outing (or come back from it) or the number of members under 21. Finding and updating files is just a matter of typing in the new information with appropriate instructions. An accounts program will help you sort out the society's cashflow problems, and add a new air of authority to the annual report—perhaps too much, as people will accept things from a computer they'd never believe from the Treasurer. And remember that Stalin started off as just a committee secretary...

If you always have a lot of letters and circulars to send out, consider laying in a computer printer and a decent word-processing program. These will turn your computer into an electronic typewriter with a mind—of sorts—and a very good memory. You type in the text, it appears on the screen and the computer commits it to memory. While it's there you can mess around with it, alter it, cut it, correct it or add whole extra paragraphs. If you want to take out the word **idiotic** every time you've used it and put in **misguided** instead, the word processor will search it out and replace it for you. When you're satisfied with the text you can feed it straight to the printer, which types it out in as many copies

The shape of things to come?

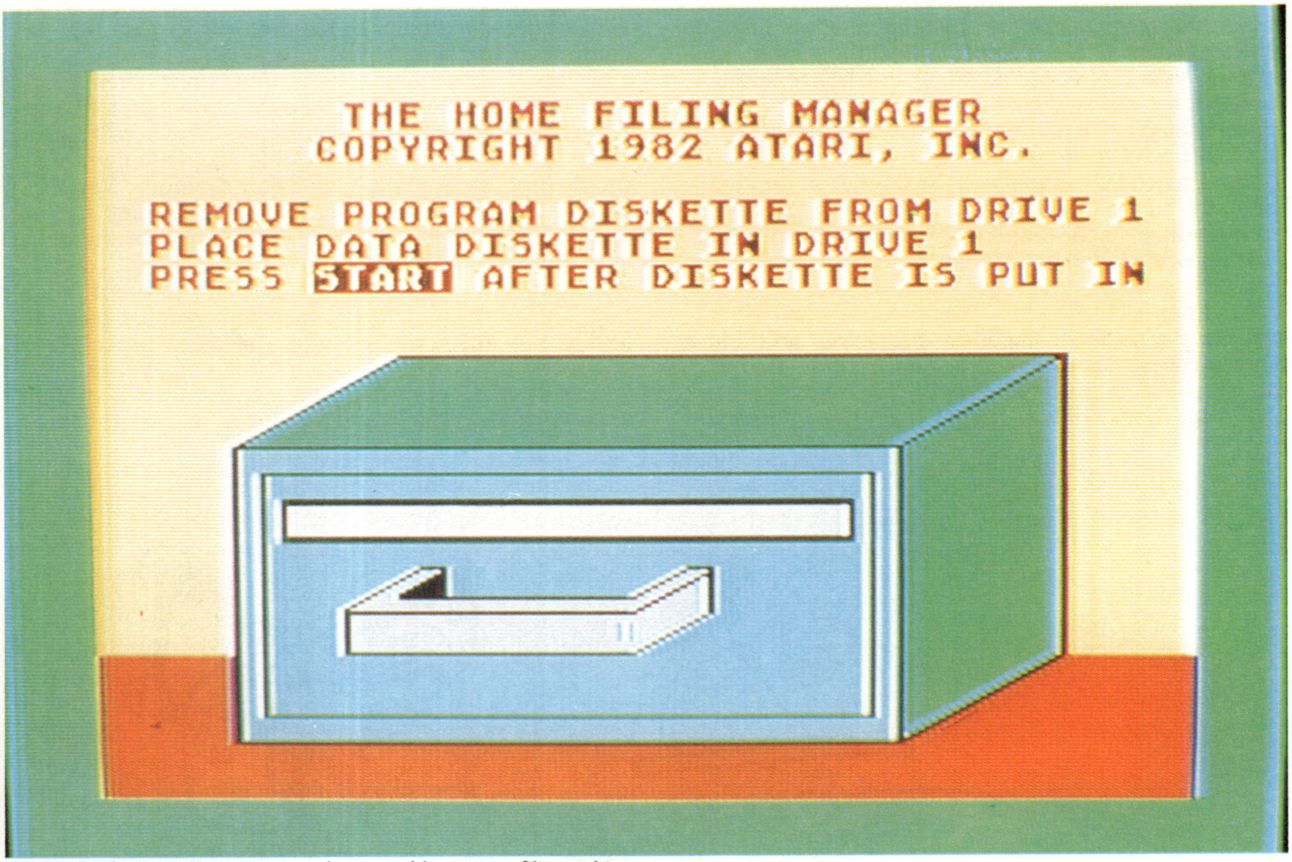


Atari's database program stresses the resemblance to a filing cabinet

as you want, or you can store it on cassette or disk. With so-called mailing facilities it will address each letter individually, or even print out labels for the envelopes. Incidentally, a word processor may also be of use to would-be novelists (which, to judge by a contest I worked on recently, covers half of humanity) saving them much paper, sellotape and cover fluid for redrafts. If you've called your hero Augustus and decide at the end that Sid would have been better, if you want to insert another dozen passionate passages in chapter 1 or switch the revelation that the butler did it from chapter 2 to the end, the word processor will speed up alterations enormously. There are even programs appearing which can check your spelling; don't argue, they've got something like the Shorter Oxford Dictionary in there...

**Lists and catalogues**

Even if you're not the society type you can still run into organising problems—if you collect things, for example. Fossils, shells, stamps, prints, beer-mats, opera records, jam jars, militaria, parking tickets, things mundane or arcane—whatever it is, if you're really serious about it, you're sooner or later going to have more of it than you can keep track of. You end up losing things, or buying needless duplicates. A quite simple database program will make a very good catalogue, usually with a self-search facility—to list all your 1931 Mauritius stamps, for example, or all the trilobites from Torquay. And even if you're not a collecting fanatic you may still acquire

A word-processor program tells its own story—but doesn't correct bad punctuation!

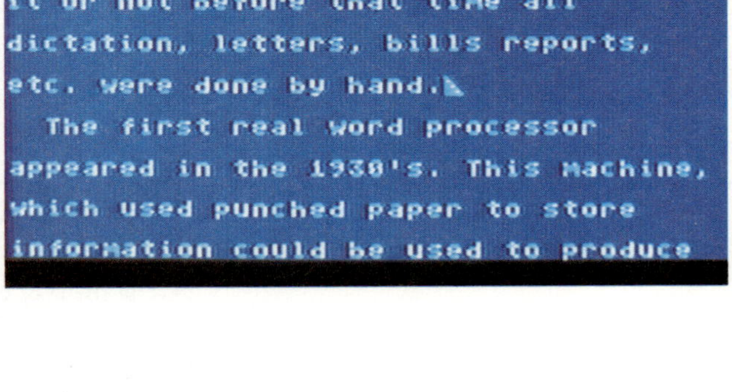

large numbers of things that need arranging—holiday snaps, for example, or recipes. On the whole, I would say it isn't worth buying yourself a computer for these uses alone—but it's a very good way of getting extra value from something you mainly want for fun.

## Control

So far this is one of the least common uses for home computers, but, if American experiences are anything to go by, that is due to change. Just as a computer outputs signals to control its display screen or its printer, it can—with the aid of a suitable matching device known as an **interface**—be used to control anything you can switch on and off. This is how those robot arms that build cars are controlled; in fact, you can even buy miniature arms for your computer, but their uses are largely educational (though one commercial chess computer uses an arm to move pieces on the board!). You can, though, already buy a specialised interface for the little Sinclair ZX-81 which lets it control a quite complex model-railway layout, balancing train times and speeds against points, signals and timetables with a finesse that puts British Rail to shame. Other control applications, linked to the computer's other abilities, open up some really exciting possibilities—and not in centuries or decades, but in the next two or three years.

An analogue watch represents the passing of time by the movement of hands across a dial; a digital watch shows it as an increasing number

**Coming attractions**

You're at the office, or on holiday. Suddenly the phone rings. It's for you... 'Hello, this is your home computer,' says the smooth voice. 'Sorry to bother you, but indicators show that the deep-freeze has stopped working and is defrosting fast. What shall I do?'

'Switch off the heating in the kitchen,' you say, very slowly and clearly. The computer repeats what you have said as a check, then adds 'Kitchen heating off.' You call the emergency repair service, arrange with a neighbour to let him in, but forget to tell the computer. So a little while later you get another call, telling you that the kitchen burglar-alarm connection has been tripped, and asking if the police should be called.

Everything else I've described is possible now. Is that little scene? The answer, surprisingly enough, is yes. All the computer abilities it implies—monitoring the freezer and the alarm system, controlling the heating, using the phone, generating speech and recognising it—are implemented on home computers now. In America you can buy all the necessary equipment over the counter, and you will soon be able to do so in Britain and elsewhere. Admittedly, it is harder to make all the separate abilities work together as smoothly and reliably as they do in our example, but that is only a matter of time and design; the technology is there for the taking. Certainly some of the American equipment falls not far short of this level already. Control and monitoring are fairly simple; instrument signals that would normally operate dials (analogue form) are translated into digital form so the computer can understand them, and it outputs digital control signals which other devices translate back into analogue form, operating switches. Speech generation is more difficult, but readily available; words are built up out of phonetic 'bricks' or individually generated from memory. They usually sound like undernourished Daleks, but improvements come all the time; the BBC microcomputer can generate the smooth tones of a well-known TV newsreader! Speech recognition is probably the least advanced form; however, programs exist which can teach a home computer to recognise a certain number of words spoken in the same way by the same voice, and there is already at least one calculator for blind people on the market which both 'hears' spoken figures and instructions and speaks the results, quite clearly. Accuracy is said to be very high, so again, it seems to be only a matter of time. As for using the phone, home computers are already doing that extensively in the USA, and soon will be in Britain (though it helps that on America's commercialised phone services local calls are usually free!). They use an oddly-named device called a **modem**, which you will learn more about in chapter 4. The possibilities are endless, because at the other end of phone lines are giant macrocomputer systems to which you can hook up your own little machine. You can buy extra computer capacity and time to deal with knotty problems; you can 'download' information or programs from their databases into your own machine, and also send or receive 'electronic mail'—messages deposited in the database and accessible only to the addressee's computer, which displays or prints it out for him. British journalists are already sending their copy across the Atlantic this way. Such databases provide the same kind of teletext information service as the BBC's **Ceefax** or ITV's **Oracle**—'pages' of news, weather, travel reports, theatre and cinema programmes, recipes,

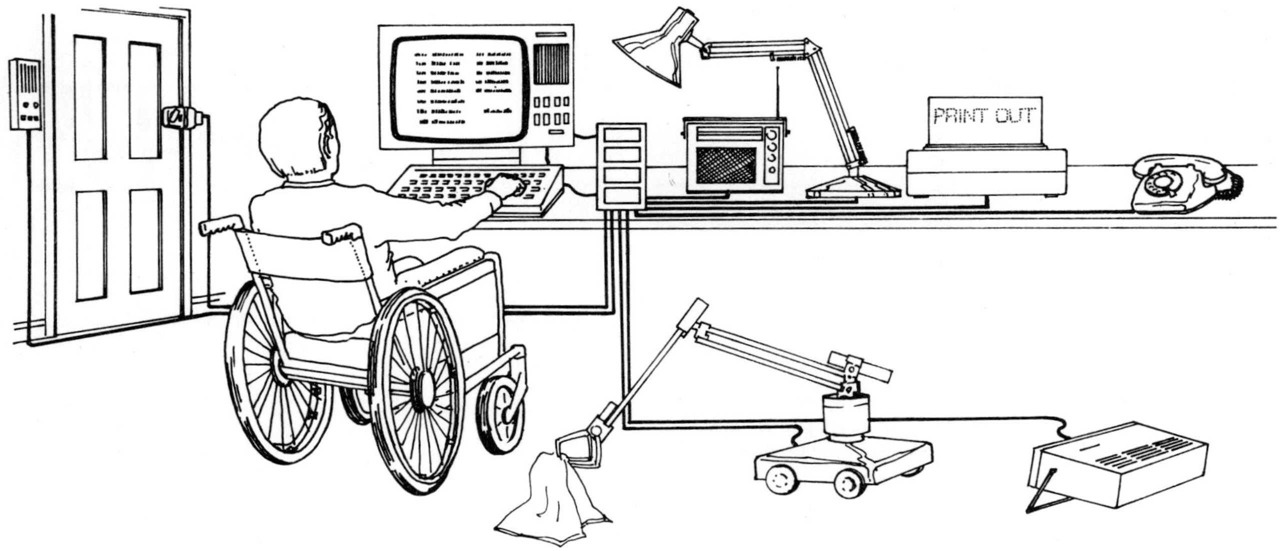


Control attachments will allow the severely disabled to operate all kinds of devices—ultimately even robot arms—from microcomputer keyboards, even to work via a telephone link. If, that is, the money can be found ...

stock-market information and so on—and also 'electronic magazines', multi-page publications renewed at intervals. British Telecom's **Prestel** service was the first such service in the U.K., but, oriented towards business users, it has so far been too expensive for home operators. Now that cheaper modems are appearing and that British Telecom is being more reasonable about licensing them, though, Prestel and a business concern are setting up the reduced-rate **Micronet 800** system. A well-known electronics magazine has also established one, and a computer company is also planning to. In the USA databases such as The Source have proved to be excellent business operations, so no doubt many more will follow.

## Roll your own

In all of this, I hope you've found some possibility that interests and excites you. But remember—I have deliberately limited myself to things which are available off the shelf, or soon will be. If you have some particular need or concern which isn't covered, consider whether you could write a program to do it for yourself. The chances are that you could, but if your nerve or time fail you, why not write to a computer magazine and ask? It always seems to me that there are more programmers around than ideas. If somebody reads your plea he may be moved to try writing what you need—especially if he thinks there may be some commercial demand for it. But I still think you are better trying it yourself, if you have the time to learn, because in the end you are the best judge of what you want. The prospect shouldn't scare you. Computers are complex, but not impossible to understand; anyway, they seem to be getting simpler all the time—there are even programs which write programs now, in answer to a few questions. Read on, and judge for yourself.

# 3. How on earth do they think?

The short answer is, they don't. The best a computer can do is mimic the processes of human thought, much the way a parrot mimics human speech. The reproduction may sound perfect, but there isn't a shred of real awareness behind it; the parrot knows nothing of the real meaning in the sounds it makes. A computer, as we shall see, can only reproduce so much of human thought as can be expressed in mathematical relationships; the real surprise is just how much **can** be. But that depends on the person programming it; his is the real intelligence in a computer, and the only mind you ever see at work. However, we shouldn't underestimate the computer. If it can only reproduce a part of our thinking processes, it can carry out that part far faster, far more accurately, in far greater amounts and without getting bored or tired. So what we really ought to be asking is—what makes them **appear** to think?

It's debatable whether you really need to know the answer. To have fun with a computer, as with a car, you don't need to know how it works, just how to make it work. But even a rough and simplified idea of how cars work will make you more at home in them, aware of their strengths and limitations, and so a better and more adaptable driver. So it is with computers. You can begin with a simple outline like this; the rest, if you want it, you will acquire later.

## First principles

The answer to our new question is also pretty simple. The operating principle of any computer, whatever the size, is one you use a hundred times daily without giving it a thought—that of the two-state device, of which the best example is the switch. Obviously every switch has two states; it can be on—in which case current is flowing, or off—in which case it isn't. The presence or absence of something, when you think about it, is just about the simplest form of knowledge or information there is; when there's no light it's dark—and so on. A tiny scrap of information like that isn't worth much, but in sufficient amounts such scraps can be used to represent much more significant and complicated information—numbers, for example.

### Numerical information

When you think of a number you are, strictly speaking, still counting on your fingers. It's hard to handle **really** large numbers—say, 14—that way, even if you carry on onto your toes. And ears, teeth, etc. make the calculation just too complicated. So we have all agreed (didn't anyone ask you?) to count up to nine fingers only, and use the tenth finger to begin a new column, representing completed double handfuls of fingers. When we come to write 'ten' down, then, we indicate that there is one (1) complete set of fingers and no individual ones (0) left over—10; fourteen is one complete set plus four more fingers, 14. When you start dealing in larger numbers you just add more columns; two hundred and fourteen equals twice ten complete sets of fingers, plus one complete set, plus four fingers. Each extra column in our numbering system represents a multiple of ten. But what if we had never got round to using our fingers? Suppose we chose to count only on eyes, ears, nostrils or anything else we've got just two of? It sounds ridiculous, just about the most awkward numbering system possible, working in columns of two, not ten. And so, from our point of view, it is. But a switch can represent it very well.

Compare the way numbers based on ten—denary, or (less correctly but more commonly) decimal—and based on two—binary—are set out in the table.

### How binary works

**decimal**

| Thousands | Hundreds | Tens | Units | |
|---|---|---|---|---|
| | | | 2 | = 2 |
| | | 3 | 2 | = 32 |
| | 4 | 3 | 2 | = 432 |
| 5 | 4 | 3 | 2 | = 5432 |

**binary**

| Eights | Fours | Twos | Units | |
|---|---|---|---|---|
| 0 | 0 | 0 | 1 | = 1 |
| 0 | 0 | 1 | 0 | = 2 (1 lot of 2) |
| 0 | 0 | 1 | 1 | = 3 (1 lot of 2 plus 1 unit) |
| 0 | 1 | 0 | 0 | = 4 (1 lot of 4) |
| 0 | 1 | 0 | 1 | = 5 (4 + 1) |
| 0 | 1 | 1 | 0 | = 6 (4 + 2) |
| 0 | 1 | 1 | 1 | = 7 (4 + 2 + 1) |
| 1 | 0 | 0 | 0 | = 8 (1 lot of 8) |

So 32 would be 100000 in binary.
Sorry, but 5432 would be a little long to print here!

Binary looks laborious, and it is. (Fortunately you don't have to work in it unless you want to!) But imagine a row of switches, one for each binary digit (or, in computer jargon, each **bit**); turn a switch on for every 1 and off for every 0, and you have an electronic representation of a number in two-state devices. These are operating together side by side, and so the number is said to be held in **parallel** form. But you could represent it another way, blipping a single switch on for each 1 and off again for each 0 as you read along the number; the bits are read in a series, and so the number is said to be held in **serial** form. These are the two ways that computers treat binary numbers.

### Non-numerical information

The computer can only handle information in binary form, and yet you will see that it can cope with anything from letters of the alphabet to swooping Space Invaders. How does it manage this? Quite simply. Letters or characters are represented by patterns of binary code; the computer handles them in this form, and they are 'translated' back again when it has finished with them. Does that sound complicated? It isn't; you may have done something very similar yourself, if you've ever used Morse code. Morse is also designed for use by a two-state device, the 'dot-dash' or 'dit-dah' telegraph key; it is sent down the line as pulses and translated back at the other end. Computers could use just about any code, but most of them (though not all) use the American Standard Code for Information Interchange—ASCII. But to the computer it's all binary.

### Handling information

The computer, then, holds and transmits the information it works with in patterns of two-state devices representing binary code. But its most important function is to **use** that information, to calculate with it—to 'process' it. The key to this is

How on earth do they think?

Acornsoft's **Peeko-Computer** program uses the BBC micro to model the action of a microprocessor with animated diagrams

the current flowing through the switch patterns; opening a switch cuts it off, obviously; and closing it again lets it flow. That current can then open or close another switch, which in turn opens or closes another, and so on, deep into a enormously complex network of interacting switches. So changing the switch pattern representing a number can change another pattern elsewhere in the circuit, and so perform a calculation. Put this onto an almost ridiculously large scale, and you have a computer. Just how large? Consider this—to carry out one simple mathematical operation, one **instruction,** the computer must perform many such pattern alterations. Some microcomputers can carry out up to a quarter of a million **instructions** a second. A decent-sized macrocomputer would sneer at that—it can cope with something around ten million instructions a second, and **its** instructions can be something like six times the size. But on the shiny case of the shop-window micro there is no indication of the frenetic activity seething below. To find it at work we must delve deep into the heart of the machine, to a little electronic component which, though it can't do much by itself, really is the computer.

**The microprocessor**

This is the famous—or notorious—'mighty micro', alternately worshipped and damned by popular prophets. Actually, it doesn't look so very

An 'X-ray' view of a typical microchip, showing the maze of connections leading to and from the actual silicon chip at its heart

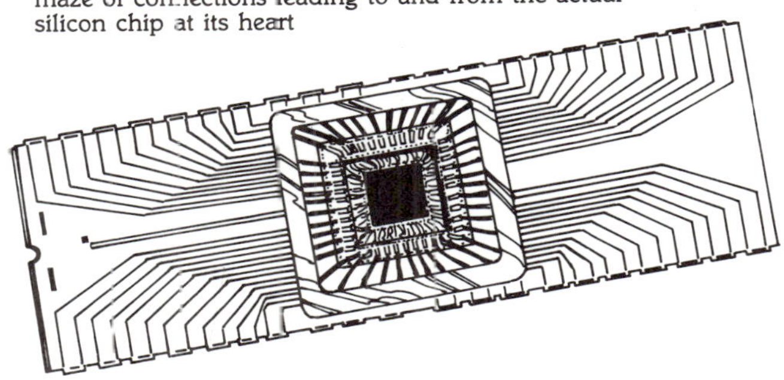

A flip-flop in its original state

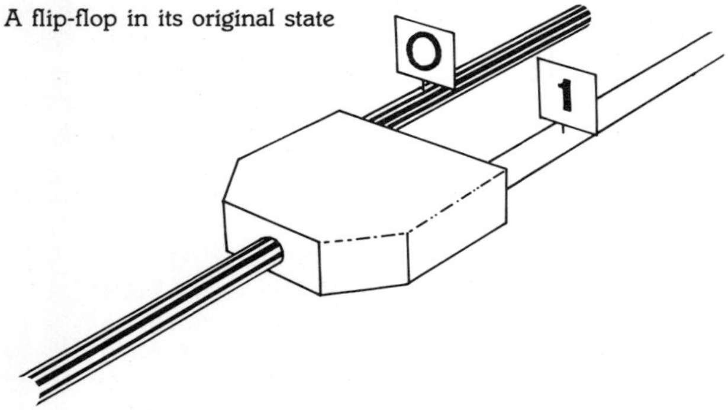


A pulse comes along:

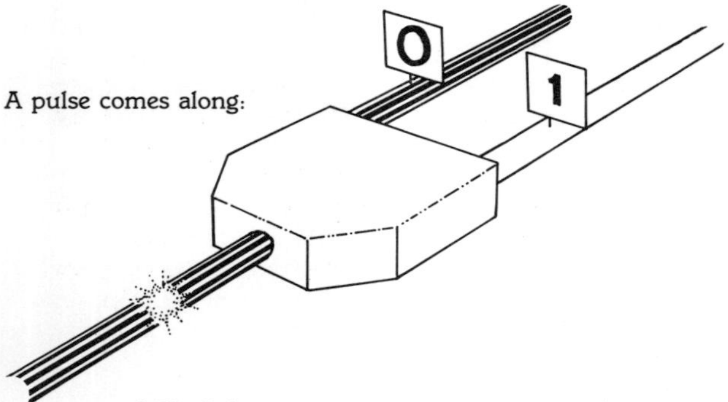


and 'flips' the current over into the other wire

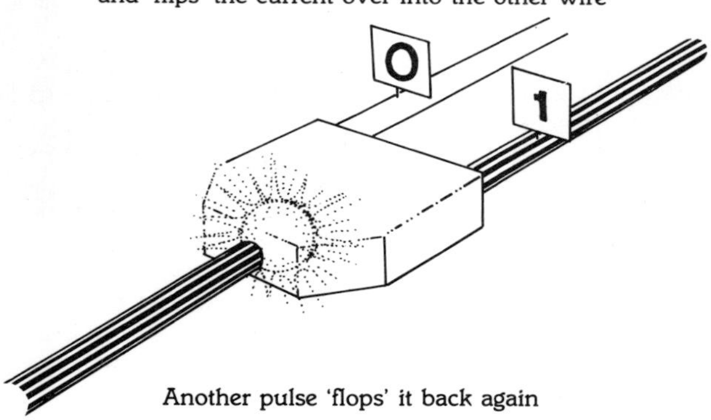


Another pulse 'flops' it back again

impressive—just a chunk of plastic an inch or so long with rows of little electrical connections along the side, like a Picasso centipede. The real microchip is even smaller, a ¼in square of thin silicon encased in the plastic to protect it and its connecting wires; to fit round the tiny edges these have to be thinner than the thinnest hairs, unable to stand unsupported. The surface of the silicon square has been etched and metal-impregnated to form a network of minute two-state devices known as 'flip-flops'. A kind of semiconductor (transistor), these switch a current along one microscopic wire when open and another when closed. On this tiny patch of silicon there are literally millions of flip-flops, shuttling minute electrical pulses back and forth, adding, subtracting, multiplying, dividing, and—perhaps most crucially—comparing. The ability to compare numbers with others is at the root of the computer's ability to choose between one course of action and another, and so make apparently intelligent decisions. You will see this at work when you try your hand at programming.

The various makes of microprocessor you find in home computers almost all handle information in groups of eight binary digits at a time; each of these eight-**bit** groups is known as a **byte**. There are several reasons for using a unit of eight; one is that you need around 256 bits—$2^8$, 2 multiplied by itself eight times—to provide code equivalents for all the characters of a standard typewriter keyboard (about 128 character codes, plus an extra 'parity' bit on the end of each one to show whether it has an odd or even number of 1 digits; this allows the computer to check for transmission errors). Simpler microprocessors, such as the ones controlling your toaster or washing machine, may only handle four bits at a time; minicomputer processors handle anything from 12 to 32 bits at a time, and macrocomputer processors from 32 to 64, or 8 bytes in all. Personal (small business) computers are now appearing with 16-bit processors, and home machines will have them in the next few years. For the moment, though, 8-bit handling is standard.

The microprocessor's main purpose in life is to perform two tasks—reading the instructions you feed into the computer, and processing the accompanying information accordingly. To do this, it is divided into two main sections, the Control Unit and the Arithmetic and Logic Unit.

**The Control Unit**

Today this is almost always part of the microprocessor chip. It has three main jobs to do; it must receive and understand instructions, transmit information needed for calculations to and from 'addresses' in the computer's memory (more about these in a minute), and control the other parts of the computer, including the ALU.

**The Arithmetic and Logic Unit**

As its name suggests, this carries out all the actual calculations, arithmetical (adding, subtracting, and so on) and logical (involving equations). Instructions and data are fed to it by the Control Unit, and it processes them in a series of rhythmical steps, regulated by the Control Unit with a 'clock' (more like a metronome, and often a separate component). Information is shuttled back and forth between the Control Unit and the ALU by a web of communicating circuits called the Internal Data Bus.

**The Instruction Cycle**

These two sections work together to carry out each

instruction in four stages. First, the Control Unit starts at a memory 'address' which contains the instruction, or part of it, in the form of a byte-length number. This first byte it sends to its instruction register, a storage point in which it triggers off signals that select one of the processor's range of operations—calculating something, say, or shifting data from one address to another. In the third stage it performs the set operation. In the fourth stage the Control Unit 'looks' to see whether it should go on to the next address or, if there is a 'jump' command, move to another address somewhere else.

**Memory**

That cycle doesn't look very complicated—but you have already seen how many times it can be carried out every second. You couldn't possibly feed information to the processor fast enough; it has to have it where it can go and get it by itself, in a form it can already use, since it can only handle such tiny scraps at one go. For this, a different kind of microchip is needed, the memory chip.

This is made in more or less the same way, but its microminiature circuits have only two, rather passive, functions—to hold binary information, and to mark where it is held. It is easier to understand how if you think of a memory chip, or series of chips, as a vast block of pigeonholes, the kind you used to see in post offices, ticket offices and—so they tell me—betting shops. Each pigeonhole holds two binary numbers—one permanently, as a label or 'address' number, and the other a piece of information. Oddly enough, the information number can only be 1 byte—8 bits—long, while the reference number is twice that length, 16 bits or 2 bytes. This looks strangely top-heavy, like a South American army with a thousand colonels and a hundred corporals, but in fact it makes sense. Memory capacity depends more on how many pigeonholes you have than how much they hold—what use are large amounts if you can't organise them? If the reference number was only 8 bits long you could only have enough numbers for $2^8$ addresses; with 16 bits you get $2^{16}$ addresses—which, since you haven't got your computer yet, works out at 65,636. In practice that means you can store around 64 thousand pieces of information—64,000 bytes, 64 kilobytes, 64K for short. A two-byte address is as much as an 8-bit processor can reasonably handle, so 64K is the practical maximum memory size for home computers at the moment. There are tricky ways of increasing it, such as switching between two memory units using the same addresses, or adding a second microprocessor, but these tend to be rather cumbersome. In practice it is quite a generous amount, even though it has to cover the computer's whole memory capacity, and this has more than one job to do. It takes a certain amount of information to run a computer and to let you put in your programs in the most convenient forms (things we will be looking at in later chapters) and therefore a certain amount of memory has to be allocated to hold this. It would be infuriatingly slow if you had to feed this in every time you switched the machine on, so the computer's memory contains two main kinds of memory microchip.

**RAM**

In the first, the Control Unit can 'write' in information, 'read' out information already there, or change it. This is known as Random Access Memory—**RAM**, one of the commonest bits of jargon flung at you. RAM is the space available for all the things **you** feed into the computer, the information and instructions that make up programs. However, the computer will often need to 'borrow' chunks of it for special functions such as very detailed 'high-resolution' graphics—and these chunks of memory aren't always small. There are two main kinds of RAM chip: **static** RAM holds information as long as the power is on, but gets rather warm. Large memories often need heatsinks, and even cooling fans. **Dynamic** RAM 'rewrites' itself continuously, needing more complex support circuitry but running cooler. Most home computers are supplied with less RAM than they can handle, to keep the price low, but with provision for expansion.

**ROM**

From the second kind of chip the Control Unit can only read what was put in the pigeonhole when the chip was made, a fixed pattern that remains after the power is turned off. ROM, Read-Only Memory, is used to hold information that goes with the machine—its **operating system**, which regulates its internal workings, and the translation system—known as an **interpreter**—for the information you feed into RAM. At one time you would have had to feed this in in binary 'machine code', but now the interpreter lets you feed in formalised commands. These are exactly like the orders an army drill sergeant shouts at his men—they don't describe in detail what he wants them to do, they just make the men remember a short sequence of actions they have learned beforehand. Each of the memory-jogging words—**mnemonics**, a name to rattle your false teeth—triggers off the interpreter to pass on a certain sequence of machine-code instructions. These systems of mnemonic commands are known as computer languages, and the best-known and most commonly used one is BASIC. We'll be looking at them in chapter 6.

**PROMS and EPROMS** These are nothing to do with concert halls. They're a strange kind of chip—Programmable Read-Only Memory, would you believe? And Erasable Programmable Read-Only Memory? They are a way of making your own imitation ROM chips; with a special machine you can 'burn' your own information into a PROM chip, which will retain it as a fixed pattern from then on.

The EPROM is a better version; it holds the information the same way, but if you want to change it you can erase the entire chip with a mighty blast of ultraviolet light, delivered by another machine. EPROMs are useful, but a little crude, costing more and running hotter than ordinary ROM chips; you're unlikely to have much use for them until you become a real fanatic, but you may find you can buy software on them for some machines.

**Buses**

And these have nothing to do with the 35 to Livingston via Midcalder. They're the last major ingredient in the computer's 'thought' processes, the complex web of circuitry that links all the others together, just as the microprocessor's Internal Data Bus linked its sections. Besides the power bus that carries electrical current to the various components, a bus system consists of three main sections. The control bus carries instructions from the microprocessor to the memory and other parts of the system; the data bus carries information and instructions back and forward between the processor and the memory; and the address bus carries the address numbers between memory and processor. Bus systems are usually visible as systems of parallel conductors on a computer's printed-circuit board.

**The thought-recorder**

So that, then, is the rather complicated way a computer 'thinks'—a purely mathematical process. Instructions and information arrive as numbers, are stored as numbers, travel through the bus system as numbers and are processed as numbers. Secondary components, ones without which the computer could still carry on its essential function, translate terms and concepts easier for us to understand into these numbers, and back again. So a computer program, in reproducing a train of human thought as a sequence of purely mathematical operations, is really only reproducing an analogue of it, a parallel version; as the grooves on an LP reproduce not the full original sound, but something similar produced by different means. But, with very good hi-fi, it can be hard to tell the reproduction and the original apart, and the same goes for computers with good programs. There's a lot to be said for good reproductions; you can play the same song as often and to as many different people as you want without bothering its creator, leaving him free to concentrate on his next piece of work. In just the same way a computer program can capture an operation of the programmer's mind and apply it to more and larger problems than he would have the time, concentration or patience for himself. That in itself is wonderful, but the thinking is his, not the computer's; it is not a 'thinking machine', just a thought-recorder.

What the computer actually does would seem less wonderful and less useful if it couldn't do so much so quickly. In fact, it was the problem of size and complexity that dogged the early computer pioneers; the concept of the computer was around for a long time before the technology to build it. Just how long may surprise you.

## The first computers

Historians usually treat the invention of writing as man's first step towards recording things he knew—information—but there is ample evidence that he in fact developed thought-recording **mechanisms**, of a sort, first. The knowledge most vital to primitive man was that of the changing seasons and the weather patterns that changed with them, governing his hunting, gathering and fishing. In the changing patterns of the stars he had an infallible calendar, and he must have taken to checking these against a fixed reference point—originally perhaps a convenient tall tree or mountain-peak on the horizon. Later, though, our ancestors built their own reference points. Archaeologists disagree about the details, but there is little doubt that most of the massive megalithic (giant stone) monuments dotted about Europe were built to embody and so record some form of astronomical information. The classic example is Stonehenge, on Salisbury Plain in England; in its original form of complete stone circles it could have been used to predict everything from new moons to solstices and even eclipses and similar rare phenomena. It was built around 4000 to 5000 years ago, long before the Romans and their

contemporaries the Druids, who were once thought to have built it. At that time writing was just beginning in the Middle East and possibly in Asia—nowhere else. Stonehenge's builders left no inscriptions.

Another and more easily recognisable 'thinking machine' dates from around the same time—but has survived in use to the present day. Probably many races used little pebbles to help them count when they ran out of fingers—the word **calculate** comes from Latin **calculi**, pebbles—but one or two had flashes of genius and strung the stones on thongs, sliding them back and forward to mark a count. Later whole rows of these thongs would be set in a frame, representing the ascending columns of a numerical system. The counting frame or abacus was doubtless invented independently all over the world, but the earliest ones seem to date from China at about the time Stonehenge was being built. In the hands of a skilled user the abacus remained the world's most efficient calculating device for many centuries; just after World War II a Japanese abacus clerk defeated an American using the latest mechanical adding machine. Only the electronic calculator is faster, and the abacus is still widely used in the East.

Those arch-bureaucrats the Romans never quite got the hang of it, probably thanks to their awful numbering system; in the wreck of their empire, Europe increasingly jettisoned this in favour of Arabic numbering, though even today Roman numerals are somehow thought more 'academic' and attractive. Perhaps, too, it hindered the development of another, even more advanced concept—so advanced that until recently nobody dreamed it had existed so early. But in the early 1970s divers exploring the wreck of a Greek ship of the 1st century AD—when Greece was part of the Roman Empire—found a mysterious lump of corroded bronze. On examination it turned out to be a box containing a system of beautifully made and elaborately intermeshed gearwheels; these turned dials with astrological symbols on them, perhaps when a date or the number of a thrown dice was entered—an ingenious fortune-telling device. But the Greeks, superb mathematicians for centuries, could have adapted that little toy into quite an advanced mechanical calculator, the kind developed by computer pioneers 1600 years later. Perhaps somebody did, but was forgotten because he never realised the full possibilities of his invention—like Hero of Alexandria, who harnessed steam power, but used it only for toys and temple tricks.

So Europe had to get by with written calculations—when enough people could write—and various wooden tallies; the term **exchequer** comes from the tally system used by the royal treasury. Only in Elizabethan times did the great Scottish mathematician John Napier invent two enormously influential calculating aids—logarithms, and 'Napier's Bones', a system of flat-sided bone or wood rods marked with numbers and the multiples of those numbers; they could be variously arranged to form tables, and long multiplications performed by adding multiples. Soon after Napier's death the English clergyman Oughtred combined these two inventions in a series of rules marked in lengths corresponding to logarithms, which could be slid against each other to carry out calculations—the first slide-rule. This, in its various forms, became the most accurate calculating device in the West until the calculator appeared.

### Mechanical computers

However, slide-rules were always too complex for the average man in the street to use for his

The original Pascaline

everyday work. In 1623 the son of a minor French tax-collector, fed-up with having to help with his father's accounts, developed a device to speed up the calculations. He saw what the ancient Greeks failed to—that ten-toothed gearwheels could be used to represent the columns of denary numbering, the tenth tooth moving the next wheel up one place, 'carrying' a number. His device had six wheels, so it could add or subtract up to 999,999; he called it the Pascaline, because his name was Blaise Pascal. He was to become one of France's greatest mathematicians and philosophers, but the machine never really caught on; it was expensive to build, and clerks feared it would put them out of work. (Does anything sound familiar?) However, mathematicians such as the German Leibnitz and the Englishman Thomas Morland took up and extended the concept, making it capable of direct multiplication and division; it became the ancestor of modern mechanical adding machines and cash registers, only now being overtaken by electronics. And the Pascaline survived as a toy; I had one myself as a schoolboy, in the lid of a pencilcase. But it was too noisy to use in exams...

All these devices may seem a long way from the microprocessor we saw. So they are—but the crucial gap is not really between gears and electronics, but between a machine that can only carry out a set calculation at a time, and one that could handle any kind of calculation, or sequence of calculations, it was ordered to. The first man to develop this concept was the British mathematician Charles Babbage, Lucasian Professor of Mathematics at Cambridge from 1828 to 1839. Annoyed by errors in printed logarithm tables, he had tried to develop a complex mechanical calculator called the Difference Engine, which could calculate them **and** print them out, avoiding human error. It failed because of the low standards of engineering in early Industrial Revolution England; Hamilton the ironmaster boasted that his steam-engines had no errors 'greater than the thickness of a shilling!' Gear systems built to such tolerances were bound to rattle and jam, and the Difference Engine never worked; the government support Babbage had received was withdrawn. He was not deterred; he had been studying the punch-card system invented by the Frenchman Jaquard to control looms, letting through only needles carrying some thread colours and holding others back; he realised this principle could be used to control the operations of a multiple-purpose calculating 'engine', activating some gear systems and not others. He began designing the Analytical Engine, so large it would have to be driven by steam. Like a modern computer, it held numbers in addressed 'registers' from which they were called by the calculating unit; numbers would be fed in on cards and results printed out. In all this he had the help and support of his wealthy mistress, Ada, Countess of Lovelace, daughter of Lord Byron and herself a notable mathematician. But the limitations which had ruined the Difference Engine held back the Analytical Engine; Babbage was literally ahead of his time, and too blind to the practical limitations of engineering. The Engine would have worked; the world's first computer might have been steam-powered. But even with modern technology it would be enormously difficult to make such a machine work reliably, far more trouble than it is worth. When Ada died young much of the heart went out of Babbage's work. By the time he died in 1871 his work was being used to improve ordinary single-purpose calculators, but no more, and he was largely dismissed.

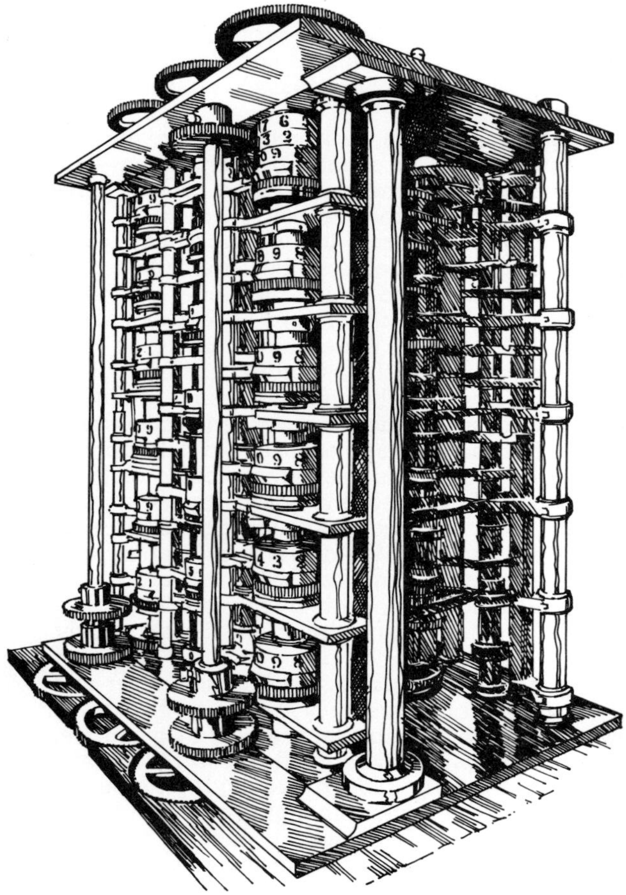
Babbage's Difference Engine

Electricity, and the transmission of information by wire, had appeared on the scene by then. In the rapidly expanding U.S.A. horrified census officials realised that they would not have finished collating the 1880 results by the time the 1890 census came round, and held a contest to develop a faster way of sorting out the information. This was won by the inventor Herman Hollerith, who adapted the Jacquard system to telegraph technology, so that punched cards made or broke electrical contacts and the result moved needles on dials. His device sorted the entire 1890 census results in only six weeks!

Hollerith's Tabulating Machine Company sold these devices all over the world, and before his death in 1929 had grown into the International Business Machine Corporation—IBM for short.

**Electrical and electronic computers**

Scientists and mathematicians, meanwhile, continued to try and improve mechanical calculators, and ran into the same problems that had brought down Babbage. The interaction of gear on gear was simply too crude for the complex systems they needed, and in the 1930s a professor at Massachusetts Institute of Technology called Vannevar Bush replaced some sections of his mechanical system with networks of electronic valves. Bush's machine inspired a similar one at Manchester University in England, and over the next few years the concept of the computer was taken increasingly seriously, particularly as binary numbering was adopted. This was only one of the many discoveries the German engineering student Konrad Zuze had to make for himself; working almost completely on his own, in his parents' house, he constructed a functioning computer, first using semi-mechanical relays as switches, and later valves. He became one of the pioneers of the post-war commercial computer industry.

But it was Howard Aiken, a mathematician at Harvard, who first looked back at Babbage's work and realised that electronics could bring it to life. By contrast to Zuze, he gained the massive support of IBM to develop his Automatic Sequence Controlled Calculator; it still used relays, not electronic switches, and was immensely unreliable when completed in 1944. However, it worked, and vindicated Babbage a century after his own design had appeared.

A number of American designs have been cited as the first true electronic, as opposed to electromechanical, computer, but it now appears that **Colossus**, developed in Britain in 1943, has that honour. It was the last in a line of codebreaking machines developed by a secret research unit at Bletchley; it used 2000 valves, and read information off punched paper tape carried by what looks like salvaged bicycle gears! Still, it broke German codes effectively enough to have remained a Government secret until the 1970s. Post-war American designs such as ENIAC and EDVAC were certainly larger, and were the direct ancestors of the first commercially-produced computer, UNIVAC-1, in 1947. By the 1950s large electronic firms such as IBM and Ferranti were selling large valve-based computers to government and industry. These machines were enormous affairs, unreliable by modern standards, drinking huge amounts of power and generating considerable heat; they needed a large support staff and programming team, and were far beyond the reach of even the wealthiest private individuals. It was the advent of the transistor, and with it the integrated circuit, that both increased the computer's power and shrank it in size—right down to that ¼in silicon square.

To begin with, transistors were wired individually into circuits like the valves they replaced—an advance in itself because they were far smaller, used only a trickle of power and generated hardly any heat. But very early on it was realised that you could put more than one transistor on the same chunk of silicon, **and** the necessary electrical conductors as well, producing a more compact and reliable circuit for almost the same price. Other researchers managed to shrink the transistors themselves to tiny film-like layers. When the two techniques met, the first 'integrated circuit' chips were produced. But the basic unit cost of producing a chip is much the same whether it carries 20 or 20,000 components, so research was geared to increasing the number that could be fitted on and so getting better value. This led to a chip with enough transistors to act as an independent, self-contained processing device; the first was produced by the Californian company Intel in late 1971. It carried about 2,250 components; today's chips can carry around 100,000 transistors (though they have become so small as to make the concept of any 'individual' transistor rather meaningless), and that rate of progress looks like carrying on to the theoretical limits—the point where individual components become so small that the material's electrical properties change. And that is still a long way away.

**Thoughts?**

The computer, then, is not some modern Frankenstein's creation out of nowhere, but a logical development of a train of research dating back to the 17th century or even earlier. Babbage would have understood a modern computer; so would Pascal and even Napier—the maths, anyway, though he might have been superstitious about electricity. They would all have recognised that the

The computer's 'conversational' ability is specially useful in language lessons, where it can combine simple graphics, a printed text and a speech soundtrack to let the learner use the language realistically

And now, a word from someone who should know...

computer's ability to make decisions is not 'thought' as such, because it cannot do so independently, on the basis of experience. A chess-playing computer can 'learn' by its mistakes, but only because the programmer anticipated the process for doing that and wrote it into the program. And the computer's real 'inner landscape' is one of mathematical relationships, which it will keep on processing equally happily whether they represent only maths or some wholly different kind of information. The human brain may or may not operate like a computer—there is evidence that it holds its information in much more complicated forms, perhaps related to holographic '3-D' patterns—but if so it is not one we can presently duplicate. Even quite small computers can carry on a 'conversation' indistinguishable from a human being's—but only because the programmer has anticipated all the possible moves beforehand. It is more a mark of how limited most conversations are than of the computer's power to think. Perhaps a computer may be built which is programmed to learn as we do—randomly and continually, through all our wide-ranging senses at once—and build the result into a 'personality'. It may be impressive—but behind that façade Babbage's gears will still be clicking away.

# 4. Do I need all that?

You may well ask. It's the usual reaction. You're just beginning to get interested in computers, you open your first computer magazine and you see all the glossily tempting advertisements and reviews. And in all of them the neat little boxes actually labelled 'computer' seem to be surrounded by piles of exotic gadgetry. The next thing you spot is that it isn't included in the price—in fact, some of it seems to cost as much as or more than the computer itself. So, understandably, you begin to wonder just how much you'll have to fork out to get a reasonable computer. Will those little boxes actually **do** anything by themselves? Do you really need all that extra equipment?

The short answer is yes. To get the very best out of your computer you are going to need most of it. But don't faint, or consider a second mortgage, or take up applique instead. You've seen a little of how the computer itself works; now you must see how it works in conjunction with other devices to extend its capabilities to the full. These devices are called **peripherals**, because they make up a system with the computer at the centre and themselves at the periphery, like planets round the sun in the Solar System. They extend your computer enormously, but you will need few if any to begin having fun with it; in fact, you are better off without most of them until you are more or less at home with the machine itself. You can buy them gradually, and build up your complete machine as you learn to use it—but sooner or later, to get the full value of what you've spent on your computer, you must expect to spend more. To understand why, consider how a computer system operates—any system, from the giant macrocomputer running a factory to the Invaders machine in its canteen.

## The system

The general principles are always the same. They all take in the information you give them, process it according to your instructions, and pass the result back to you. If that makes them sound like a secretary or clerk, it's because there really is quite a close resemblance.

A clerk sits at his desk, equipped with in-tray, out-tray and a simple adding-machine or calculator. Behind him he has a bank of filing cabinets filled with information you have given him or based on work he has already done. You, as his boss, put some pages of information into his in-tray, with detailed instructions as to how he should deal with it. He reads the instructions, arranges the papers on his desk and works through them, putting any necessary calculations through his adding machine. The finished result goes into his out-tray for you to pick it up, or he sends it for typing.

A computer system consists of just the same units—desk, in-tray, out-tray, filing cabinet, calculator and even clerk. Its in-tray is an input peripheral—on home machines usually a typewriter keyboard with a few extra keys, though other inputs may be added for playing games. On this you type in information and instructions, your **program**. This arrives on the desk—the computer's main memory store. Here the clerk—our old friend the Control Unit—responds to the instructions, passing calculations through the ALU. However, like desk tops, main memory stores may not have enough room for all the information needed, and it can't be left lying around while other things are being worked on. Hence the filing cabinets, or

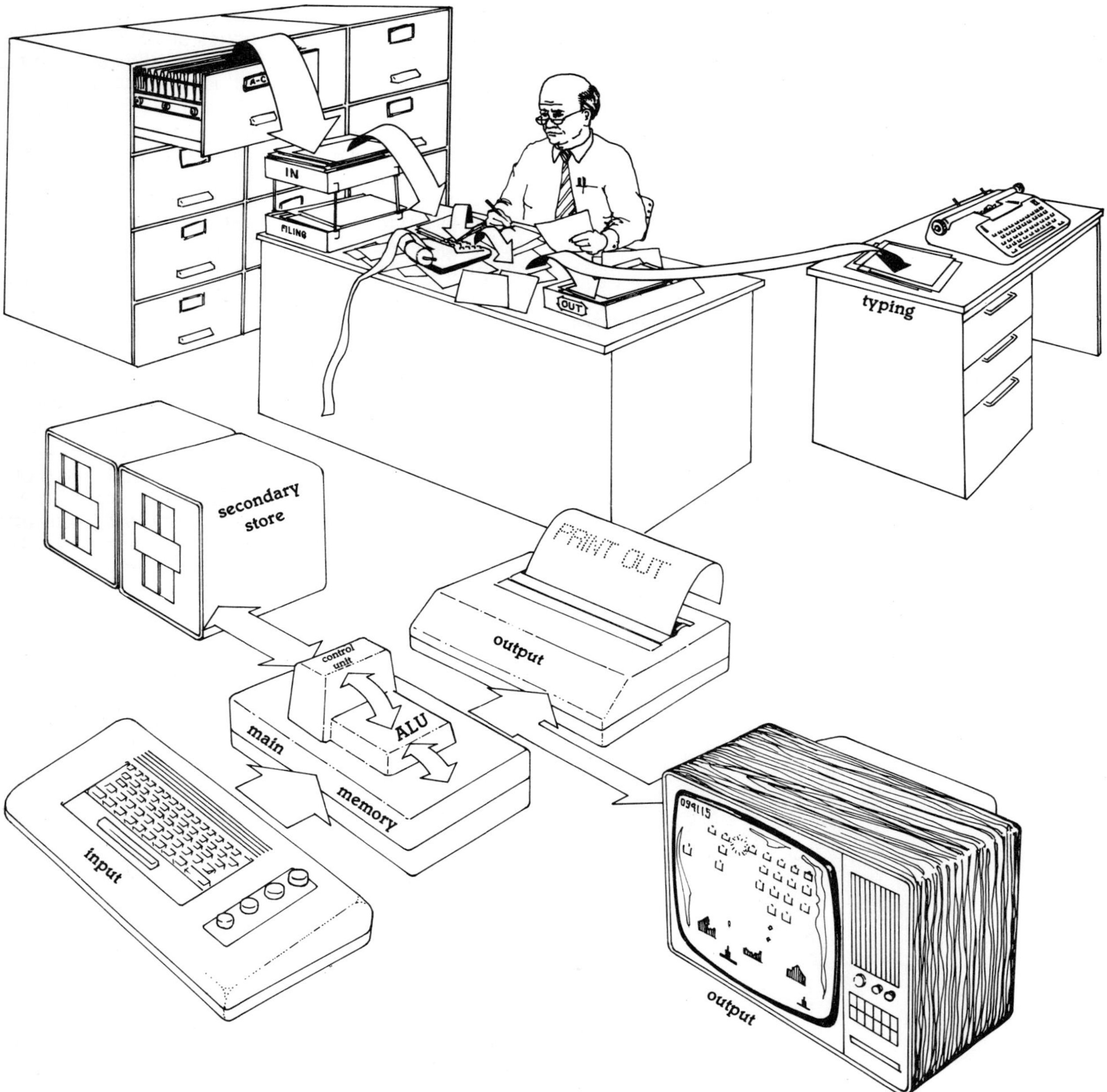


Clerk and computer—they process information in a very similar way. But the machine is more compact, faster and more versatile—try playing **Invaders** with a clerk!

backing store. When ordered to, the computer can pull more information out of these, or file some away for future reference, clearing the desk for the next stage of its job; it can also file away a copy of the results it passes to its out-tray, an output peripheral. On a home machine this is generally a cathode-ray screen, kindly provided by your own TV set. The computer's equivalent of a typing pool is another output peripheral, a teleprinter it controls directly to type out a 'hard copy' of its results for you.

These, then, are the main elements of a computer system, its 'nuts and bolts', or, in computer jargon, its **hardware.** The heart of it is obviously the clerk, adding machine and desk—processor and main memory, often called the Central Processing Unit, CPU for short—and it is this which fills all those little boxes, generally with an input peripheral, a keyboard, on top to make a neat typewriter-like unit. This is what you get when you buy your basic home computer.

And this, with a lead simply plugged into the

aerial socket of your TV set, is all you need to put in information and get it back duly processed; the information can be anything from complex maths to the firing command for your anti-Invaders laser. But the CPU can only get its information via the keyboard; it can't remember very much of it, and that only as long as the power is on; and it can't print it out in a permanent form. You can still play games on it, type in quite large programs, and begin to learn the BASIC language and write your own programs (see chapter 6). But to do more you will have to start expanding it into a proper system, and in this chapter you will see how you can build one up—what kinds of peripheral are available, how they work, and in what order you should think of getting them. The CPU consoles we will give a chapter to themselves, next.

## First steps

This could have been headed **First brick walls**, because you find out your first need by running headlong into the lack of it. There is nothing more infuriating than very slowly and carefully typing in a fascinating program, only to find there's not enough room in the memory for the vital last two lines. Except, that is, having to type in an enormously long program every time you want to use it. These are the first two limitations you are bound to run into: how much main memory you have in your CPU console—the size of the desk top—and whether you have any secondary storage—filing cabinets—available. These will be the first two extensions you will want for your computer, and it is hard to say which you should get first; it depends how adequate your main memory is to begin with.

## Memory expansion

A home computer's main memory store consists of a series of the RAM microchips you looked at in chapter 3. Most manufacturers bring the price of their cheapest models down as far as possible by selling them with far less memory—fewer chips—than they can actually use. Just how much you get differs widely, and isn't always reflected in the price. The amount is quoted in kilobytes—4K, 16K, 32K—but like hi-fi's watts per channel ratings, this doesn't always reflect what you actually get to use. In one popular machine rated at 5K, for example, 1.5K is always used up for the computer's screen

Just some of the ways a small home computer can be extended: 1. cassette deck; 2. additional memory cartridge; 3. expansion unit (with extra memory, more inputs and outputs, a second microprocessor etc.); 4. monitor screen; 5. disk drives; 6. printer; 7. sound or speech box; 8. interface for local network (link to other computers or shared peripherals nearby—here a disk drive); 9. receiver/decoder for broadcast 'telesoftware' from TV systems such as Ceefax; 10. modem telephone link for remote network (to computers or peripherals elsewhere) or for database such as Prestel; 11. joystick; 12. full typewriter-style keyboard

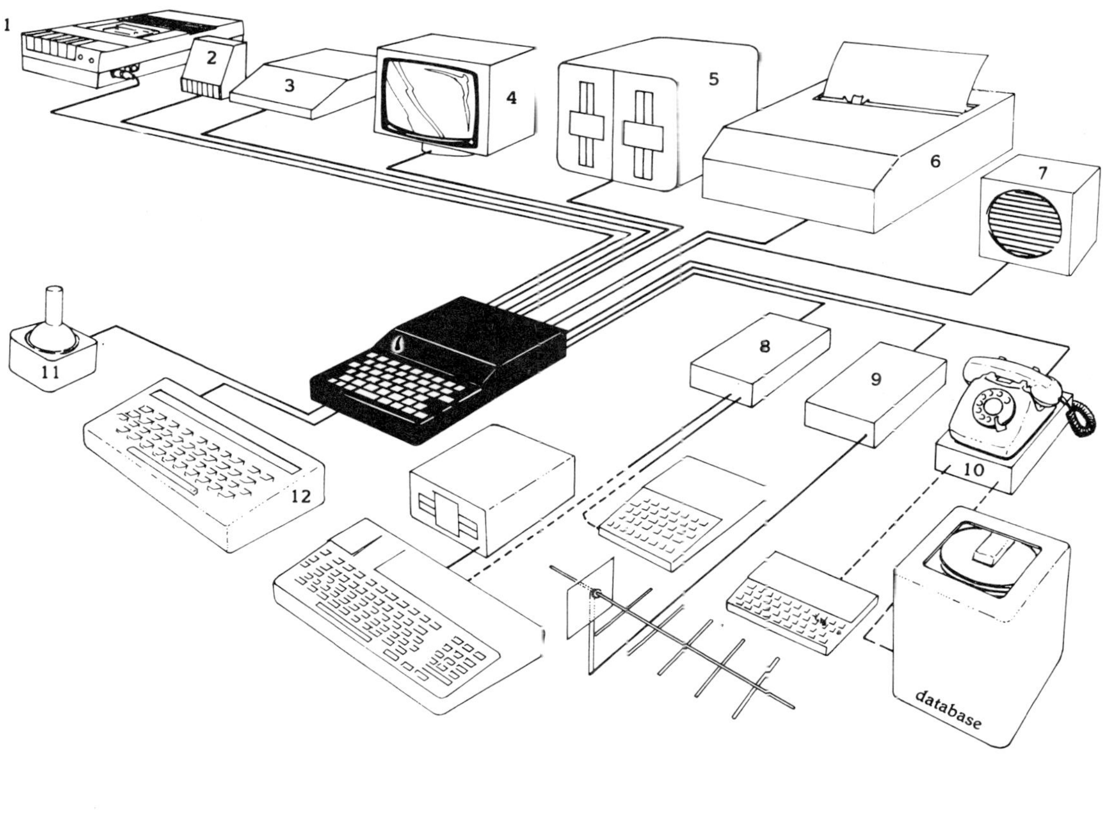

A high-quality memory-expansion cartridge—used here with a graphics pack—can greatly enhance the modest capabilities of the Sinclair ZX-81

signals; in several others user-available memory shrinks sharply when high-resolution graphics or extra or enhanced computer languages are used—in one case from 38K to 13K. What looks like a large memory may cramp your style sooner than you expect. But fortunately there are plenty of ways of adding to it, up to—and occasionally beyond—the manufacturer's limit.

**Cartridges**
This is much the easiest way, when the manufacturer provides for it. A cartridge containing the extra RAM chips plugs neatly into a socket linked to the bus system—often the same socket that takes ROM software cartridges. It is also a rather expensive way, partly because of the extra packaging, circuitry and so on, and partly because manufacturers naturally take some slight advantage of their captive market; as a rule only they make the cartridges. Another problem is unreliability, especially on cheaper machines; cartridge connectors wear, loosen or get dirty—none of which needs to be visible to start interfering with your program—and often stick awkwardly out of the case, which is not only unsightly but easy to bump into. This may be why Sinclair's ZX-81 cartridges occasionally blank out their contents; their vertical design means that even a tiny movement at the top could flex the connector considerably.

The ZX-81 is one of the few computers for which independent manufacturers make memory-expansion cartridges, many of which are claimed to be more reliable than Sinclair's. They vary considerably in quality and price, and if the extra memory is very large, sections may have to be switched in and out or 'paged' by a program instruction. Find out all you can, especially from reviews, before buying.

**Expansion boxes**
Some small computers are so cramped in design that nothing extra can be fitted on the main circuit board in their cases. You therefore have to buy an additional case, styled to match, which may contain the extra memory, or just more cartridge sockets. This is always pricey, but it often contains other facilities such as printer connections. Thankfully it seems to be becoming less common as circuit design becomes more sophisticated and compact.

**Direct upgrade**
Very often nowadays space is simply left on the main circuit board for the extra chips, which are added by the manufacturer or dealer when needed. This makes a lot of sense, if you don't mind doing without the machine for a few days—perhaps while you're on holiday. The minor inconvenience is more than made up for by the extra reliability; Sinclair have chosen this method rather than cartridges for their Spectrum. On many machines, such as the BBC micro, the upgrade also includes other facilities such as printer connections. For popular machines independent manufacturers may offer cheaper upgrades; these may be quite all right, but they invalidate your guarantee. If you get one—or any other modification by an independent supplier—during the guarantee period, make sure they will match the original guarantee **in writing** first. Make sure, too, that they really do include everything the manufacturer's upgrade does. It is also possible to buy and fit the extra chips and components yourself, but no newcomer is recommended to try it; the possibilities for damage are enormous. And you can forget your guarantee, too.

**Minimum memory**
Upgrading is seldom cheap, so you should take the cost of it into account. It often pays to get the largest version right from the word go—**if** you are sure you'll need it. 5K or less is only enough for dabbling around, but that may not matter if you're mostly going to be playing cartridge games. But if you've any doubts about that, 16K is a reasonable working minimum, and one that shouldn't strain

your pocket too much these days. Some machines under £200 have twice or three times that as standard.

## Secondary storage

This is also called backing store. The names are a bit misleading, because your filing cabinets are as indispensable as your desk; perhaps more so, because you can do more with a small main memory and plenty of secondary memory than the other way around. It gives you a far quicker and more efficient way of getting information into the main memory than typing the whole program in every time, and also a way of keeping information when you want to turn off the machine or use it for something else. Most home-computer storage systems work on the same lines. The computer reads the mass of numbers held in the memory, and, since they are in binary, it can easily translate them into a series of electronic on/off blips, like morse, and feed them out into a storage peripheral which records them, usually magnetically—just as we do with our own voices, converting them into electronic signals by means of a microphone and feeding them to a cassette recorder. In fact, guess what the simplest and commonest secondary-store device happens to be?

**Cassette recorder**

If you are lucky, your first peripheral needn't cost you a penny extra. Most home computers can store their information on an ordinary cassette deck. A connecting lead is either included with the computer or sold separately (sometimes at ridiculous prices; shop around); all you need to do is connect this. Sometimes you have to operate the recorder yourself, but on many machines the computer can do this on command, even as part of a program. However, some very reputable systems—such as Atari and Commodore—can only be used with the 'dedicated' cassette decks they themselves supply. There is some sense in this; many domestic cassette recorders are too cheaply made and badly adjusted to give good results with computers, and may not make sense of tapes recorded on other machines. However, these dedicated recorders are far more expensive—nearly twice the price of special computer-compatible machines from reliable manufacturers like Sony, which makes them bad value. And since you cannot use the machines without them you must include them in your costings.

Cassettes are a good, cheap and easy way of storing your information. As you saw in chapter 1, there is plenty of software available in this form, for just about every machine in this book. It generally

A typical floppy disk and disk drive

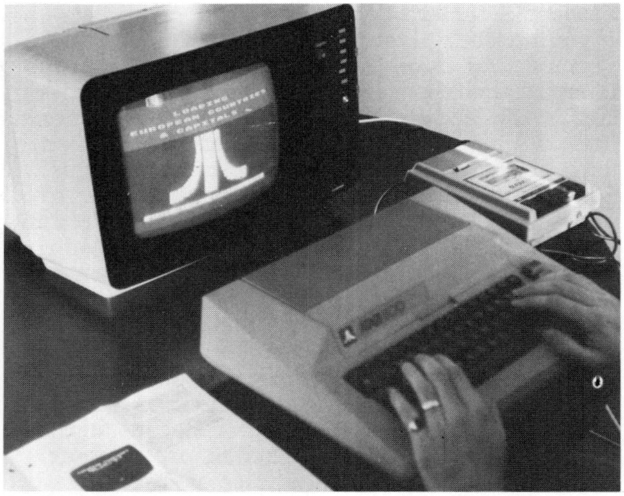

Cassette loading is slow and sometimes uncertain, so many machines give you some kind of visual indication that it is happening successfully

takes a few months from the launch of a new machine, though, for a good selection to appear on the market. But cassettes do have some serious disadvantages. First, they are extremely slow. A computer can take 15 minutes just to find a particular program on a tape, reading through all the others first with moronic care, and then take another five to load the program in, blip by blip. Second, they wear, and make the tape heads dirty and wear those out too. This can mean one extra blip being included in a program, or one left out—all you need for a really juicy disaster. These two faults reduced me to a gibbering wreck in my early computing days; my machine time was rationed to one hour, in which I had to work through a teaching program in the middle of a very long cassette. The tape was so worn that the computer kept missing the beginning of the program; I had to play it through three times before I got it, and then rocket through an hour's work in the remaining ten minutes. I felt, as you may after a while, that there had to be a better way.

**Floppy disks**

Mercifully, there is. Floppy disks are more expensive than the best cassette recorders, but coming increasingly within the reach of more serious home users.

It isn't immediately obvious that a floppy disk works on similar lines to a tape recorder. If you take one out of its protective sleeve—which you shouldn't if you ever want to use it again—you will see that it lives up to its name, looking like one of those unplayable giveaway gramophone records. Actually, though, it is a thin mylar sheet covered with magnetic oxide particles much like those on cassette tape, intended to record the blips in the same way, but on a much narrower track; it can do this because it doesn't have to be able to record sound signals as well. The surface of a floppy has several of these tracks—as separate concentric circles, not a continuous spiral like a gramophone record's grooves.

The disk is 'posted', still in its sleeve, into a slot at the front of the disk drive. Inside, the large central spindle grips the disk, and the sides of the sleeve are sucked aside. The main motor then spins the disk at high speed—usually 300 to 360 rpm—and the recording and playback head (known as the read/write head) is poked through the vertical slot in the sleeve against the disk surface. A stepper motor then moves it up and down across the tracks, following commands from the disk operating system (DOS). This is a substantial piece of software which extends the computer's own operating system, directing the operation of the disk drive or drives—how the computer 'writes' information onto disks and 'reads' it from them, how the information is laid out on the disk, 'writing' information to another disk or directly to a printer, and so on. Disk drives do not have external control keys; all the commands come via the computer. For home computers the DOS is sometimes sold as a cartridge or in ROM with the disk drives, but most often it 'resides' on disk itself; you then need a fair amount of both RAM and disk capacity to run both it and your own programs. This is one reason it is best to have more than one drive; another is that disks are rather too easily damaged and their stored information corrupted, so being able to make

simultaneous backup copies is a great advantage.

Each track on a disk is divided up into **sectors**, which are marked in one of two ways so the head can identify them as it scans the disk. The first way is by a series of holes punched around the disk centre, so-called 'hard sectoring'; the other, more flexible, way is by signals stored with the other information on the disk—'soft sectoring'. Disk drives are always either hard or soft sector, and disks are not interchangeable between the two kinds. This is only one of the many variations you have to watch out for; some disk drives have a second read/write head, so they can use both sides of a disk at once. There are two main sizes of disk, one 8in across—the standard disk—and the other 5¼in across—the minifloppy, or diskette. Sony have recently launched a 3½in 'microfloppy', and BATS, a Hungarian company, have begun marketing a 3in disk held in a stiff plastic cassette; it is still too early to say whether these will become accepted standards like their larger cousins. Disks also vary in their **density**, the amount of information they carry; this varies tremendously from type to type, and is not at all related to size—a single-density 5¼in disk may carry about 80K of information, whereas the 3½in Sony will carry nearly 219K at single density and 437.5K at double density.

The advantages floppy disks offer you are tremendous. With a cassette you have only 'serial' access to the information on it; each section of tape in turn has to be dragged wearily past the head until it comes to the right one. But at the speed the disk is moving the moving head can go straight to any sector of any track—random access—and read it off, all in a fraction of a second. If you want to demonstrate this, try finding the start of a song track on a cassette—then on the equivalent LP! You can see its tracks and move the stylus straight to them—random access again. There are other pluses, too; the capacity of a disk is much greater, as we have seen. And if you want to add something onto the end of a program you have already stored, it is much easier with a disk, which has one or two tracks to act as a 'directory' for information stored in different places on it.

But there have to be some disadvantages. Disks are far more fragile than cassettes; tiny specks of dust or dirt can corrupt them past redemption. Don't wipe your disk drives with ordinary tissues, for example; they're made with **talcum powder**! And above all, don't handle the disks; the driest skin is slightly greasy, so it'd be like wiping this book down with an oily rag. The worst disadvantage, though, is cost. You can reckon on paying £200 to £300 for the simplest disk system; adding extra ones generally costs less. It may be cheaper buying a dual drive unit, at about £350, first. In general, 'brand-name' dedicated drives like Atari's or Sharp's will cost more. You might think that disk drives are more expensive because they're harder to build than cassettes, but at least one manufacturer claims they're actually easier! The main motor, for example, only has to spin a light disk one way at a fixed speed, instead of two heavy tape reels at varying speeds. The extra cost is partly the result of lower demand; as demand increases the price is likely to fall. So you'll be perfectly well off starting with a cassette just now, getting the hang of your machine and biding your time; either the price will fall, or you'll find yourself getting a lot more for the same money. As with so much else in the computer market it never hurts to wait.

However, if you have already hurled your cassette recorder out of the window in a fury, don't despair. There is a halfway house, a godsend to poor home users like us when it first appeared a few years ago, but less popular since the price of disks began to come down. However, interest is now reviving.

**Stringy floppies**

These are also called 'floppy tapes', though there is nothing especially limp about them. Both names suggest something between disk and cassette, and that about sums them up. They are small, superfast tape transports carrying miniature cassettes called 'wafers'—full of especially strong and hard-wearing tape that travels past the head at high speeds. You still don't quite get random access, but they read through the tape so fast that that matters much less; the capacity is lower, but they can be operated by the computer as easily as a cassette deck. There are several different systems, among them the American Exatron and Aculab drives for TRS-80 machines, the Hobbit system for BBC machines, Sinclair Microdrives, using an endless tape-loop for faster access, and the new Texas drive for their 99/2. Capacity varies, but is not far short of smaller disk systems, and the 'wafers' are often less fragile. However, at the moment they are most use for storing your own data; I know of no commercial software currently available on floppy tape. The Sinclair and Texas systems may well attract some when they are established. Also, not all systems are that much cheaper than disk systems of similar capacity; compare what is available before you buy.

**Exotica**

These are the main kinds of secondary store you will want to think about adding to your computer. But there are others, at the moment mostly for the 'rich and strange' with whom this book isn't concerned. However, as their prices also seem to be beginning to fall, you should at least have some idea what they are.

**Hard disks**

These operate on broadly similar lines to floppies, but the magnetic coating is carried on a platter of stiff plastic. Because it doesn't flex this can be rotated at tremendous speeds, and the whole operation made much more precise. The read/write head doesn't actually touch the disk surface, it glides over it at about .001mm up—a feat which has been compared to flying Concorde along the M1 a metre above the road. On that scale a hair or dust-mote counts as a double-decker bus coming the other way, so hard disks have to be hermetically sealed into a container, flushed out and filled with inert gas. All this allows the head to access much finer tracks, and so cram more information onto the disk surface. The little 8in hard disks developed for use with small computers can hold as much as 26 million bytes—26Mb. It all costs money, of course—thousands rather than hundreds. But already a 3Mb 5in drive is available for under £1000. And that is what quite small computers cost only a few years ago...

**Bubble memory**

Unlike the other storage media we've looked at, this isn't any kind of cousin to tape recording. Binary information is recorded not as blips, but as the presence or absence of bubbles created electromagnetically in a special substance. It behaves very much like ordinary computer memory, except that it can be added to or erased instantly, without all the kerfuffle of EPROMS. It was developed as a cheap substitute for disks, but mass-production problems have kept the price higher. Since it can be sealed into a case and has no moving parts, though, it is ideal for use in conditions such as extreme heat, cold or dust, that would ruin ordinary drives. It is also relatively slow, since access to information is not random. But it is compact and tough, and worth watching out for if they ever get the price right for home users.

## Interfaces

Because secondary storage is such an essential part of a computer system, home computers are usually designed so that cassettes and disks can be attached quite directly, often by just plugging in a cable or cartridge. But that is less often the case for other peripherals in a system; they all have their own ways of handling data, doing different things with it at different speeds, and operating with very different levels of voltage. They cannot be connected up directly to the computer's bus system; there has to be an intermediate point at which these conflicting methods are reconciled, and information passing through is rendered into the form it must have to continue its journey. These points are known as **interfaces**, and they generally consist both of hardware and software. On home computers you don't need to think much about the interfaces for the keyboard (also a peripheral, remember) and cassette deck, because they are usually built into the console; so are disk and printer interfaces, sometimes, though these often come with expansion boxes. Very often these will only match the manufacturer's equipment, though; for anyone else's both computer and peripheral will need one of the standard interfaces. A very common one for printers is the **Centronics** interface, a parallel connection made popular by the printer company Centronics; many computers now have this fitted as standard in the CPU console. The commonest standard, though, is the **RS-232** interface, which carries information serially (as a sequence of blips, remember, instead of in parallel like the Centronics—side by side along several wires) and so relatively slowly; it is therefore seldom used with disks, whose performance depends on a high baud rate, but is ideal for printers, terminals (separate VDU screen and keyboard units) and **networking**—communication between computers, allowing them to share the use of large-scale peripherals such as hard disks or printers. Networking has obvious applications in business and education, but fewer for home users at the moment. Commodore developed a much faster parallel interface system, IEEE-488, which they use for their peripherals; it has been widely adopted for scientific instruments used with computers.

## Modems

We saw in chapter 2 that computers can communicate via ordinary phone lines. Telephone technology is pretty primitive, and accuracy is more important than speed over interference-filled public lines. The RS-232 standard is most often used, therefore, to link the computer to a device called a **modem**. This is not some term in Old High Glagolitic, it is a contraction of **mod**ulator and **dem**odulator. This 'modulates' the relatively weak computer signal into pulses that will carry clearly through the phone network and 'demodulates' incoming signals. With a modem attached to the line (via a phone socket) at each end, computers can communicate cheerfully across half the world. Until recently modems were—like many other peripherals—hideously expensive and not generally licensed for use on British public lines; instead you had to use a clumsy device called an **acoustic coupler**, with two rubber cups which clamped like an automatic milking machine over the earpiece and mouthpiece of a telephone handset, and transformed the computer signal into something loud enough to pass through the incredibly crude microphone and speaker of the handset. Now things seem to be changing, as companies—in particular Oric—are beginning to produce modems at more realistic prices, and British Telecom are making it easier to get them licensed.

## Printers

These are peripherals you may find yourself wanting even before disks; you may or may not need extra interfaces. However you store your information, you can't read it yourself. The computer has to read it for you, and translate it into characters on the screen. All very well, but how do you send a copy to a friend, or get a frameable record of an attractive graphic design, or get a

A popular model of dot-matrix impact printer, opened up to show the paper carriage and print head (left)

written record of complex accounts? You will soon find sitting by the screen with pencil and paper a bore, especially when copying your brilliant thousand-line program; make one small mistake and it's rubbish when you've typed it all in again. The answer to all this is a printer—and, if you're careful, it needn't be too pricey an answer.

Computer printers are similar to teleprinters, printing letters, numbers and graphics characters onto paper in response to the signals the computer generates. But there the similarity ends; manufacturers have found an amazing number of ways of getting the letters onto the paper. They divide, though, into two main methods, each of which has its advantages and will give you radically different results.

**Dot-matrix**

This is the commonest way less expensive printers work. It may also be the oldest; I have this theory that Sherlock Holmes invented it one day while shooting his 'patriotic VR in bullet pocks' on the living-room wall at 221b Baker Street, because it forms letters on the same principles. The print head—equivalent of an ordinary typewriter's bars or golf-ball element—is a bunch of needles which are flicked forward electronically to make dots on the paper. These dots build up each letter within a rectangle of dots—a **matrix**; the more dots in the matrix, the clearer the printed character. The commonest matrix size is 5 × 7—which doesn't mean the head is a rectangle of 35 needles! That would be fiendishly difficult to control. Instead, a vertical row of seven needles travels across the page, triggering very rapidly five times to make up each character. Larger—and usually more expensive—matrices are commonly 7 × 9 and 9 × 12. The smaller size cannot generally form the 'tails' or descenders of letters such as g and y below the line; it has to shift them up into the box, which looks very peculiar. The larger printers have 'true descenders'; one or two smaller machines fudge it

How a dot-matrix print-head forms letters

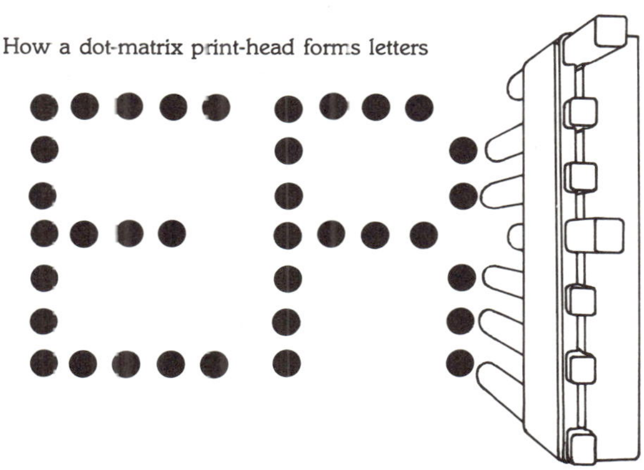

A typical inexpensive printer, using a dot-matrix print-head on thermal paper

by shifting the paper up a little and going over the line again, which also allows them to underline. Some printers can manage bold print by going over the line again shifting the print head very slightly out of line; some very sophisticated dot-matrix printers use this method to fill in between the dots and produce very clear text.

Speeds vary as widely as abilities, and are often affected by the use of things such as underlining facilities. The computer can generally output information faster than the printer can type it, so most machines have a kind of limited memory, called a **buffer**, in which the information queues up. On 'bi-directional' machines the print head prints in both directions ('mentally' reversing the line) which speeds things up. But even the slowest dot printer is far faster than most human typists, so you may not be too worried about that. Even the way the needles actually make the dots varies; some by striking an ink ribbon against paper like an ordinary typewriter, others by heating the needles to produce blue dots on metal-impregnated paper, and yet others by electrostatically burning a metallic coating off special paper. The second and third ways sound fearsome, but in fact are cheap and (relatively) quiet, and so favoured for less expensive machines. The special paper, though, is expensive, and both processes make rather a strange smell, especially if used for too long.

Cheapest of all are printers that use only one or two print needles, scanning across a whole line of type and producing the top dots of each character, then shifting the paper up a dot and producing all the ones in the next row, building up all the characters in the line from the top down. This is rather crude, and works best on narrow paper, but it simplifies the printing process immensely; most printers under £100 use this system.

Dot-matrix printers produce text which is generally clear enough but unlovely and, in large quantities, rather a strain to read. Only the best ones produce anything which could rival an ordinary typewriter, and they are expensive. But cheaper ones are fast and flexible enough for everyday use, and those with a graphics capability can dot you out a very creditable 'drawing' of just about anything you can put on the screen. These will set you back £200 or more; if all you want is program print-outs and the occasional simple graphic, the under-£100 printers such as the Sinclair (dedicated, but adaptor kits for other machines can be found) will be all you need.

**Character printers**
If, on the other hand, you want to produce superbly clear typewriter-quality copy and will never want anything like a picture with it, you should look at the character printers on the market. These use typewriter-style ribbons and print elements—golf-balls, 'thimbles', and most of all daisy-wheels—to produce text, always on ordinary paper. Some of them, in fact, are electronic typewriters with just an interface added; be careful of these, because they are not really meant to stand up to the constant heavy punishment a computer gives them, typing faster than a human and never stopping for coffee. If you only need high-grade copy occasionally, you **could** buy one of them **and** a cheaper dot printer for the price of a more robust character machine—my own solution—but be sure that fits your needs. Some purpose-built character printers are now appearing for around £400, which is a tremendous drop from the old prices.

Character printers are not nearly as fast as dot-matrix machines—around 60 characters per second at most, and sometimes as little as 10 or 12, whereas dot machines manage anything from 80 to 200. They are generally extremely noisy, and with that goes a tendency to shake themselves apart. A really good one will still set you back about £1000.

**Paper and ribbons**
Both types of printer work too fast to use ordinary paper easily without a special feeding mechanism, which is pricey. Instead the paper comes on rolls or in fanfolds, flat sheets linked by perforated end folds so they open out continuously, like a fan. The paper may be advanced by friction alone, as in an ordinary typewriter, but at high speeds traction or sprocket feed, locking into holes along the edges of the paper, is more stable. The paper looks less neat, but produces better aligned print and fewer jams and misalignments, which turn printer into paper shredder. Thermal and electrostatic papers usually only come as rolls, costing more than plain paper. For plain paper, though, printer ribbons have to be counted into the cost; some of these are ridiculously over-priced, and though this is less common you should check carefully before buying.

**Plotters**
If you will chiefly want to copy graphics, and seldom if ever text in any quantity, you could consider getting a plotter. The computer signals that control print-heads can also control the movement of pens across paper, to draw continuous lines and not strings of dots; more than one pen can be used, to produce multi-coloured designs. Plotters have many scientific and business uses, and the prices tend to reflect this; however, models priced for the home market are beginning to appear. One four-colour model already sells for less than £100 in Japan. Remember, though, that a plotter produces text relatively slowly and is generally less robust than a printer.

**Teletypes**
One or two firms sell 'reconditioned' office teletypes as 'suitable for conversion' for use as a computer printer. One or two knowledgeable enthusiasts have actually managed to do this, but the result is still large, power-hungry and unbelievably noisy, not to mention unreliable. Personally I would avoid them like the plague. You have a very large selection of purpose-built printers to choose from, made by firms such as Epson, Oki, Centronics, Seikosha, Amber, Anadex and the computer manufacturers themselves; you can go from 20 characters per line to 80 or even 132, over an amazingly large range of print methods and paper types. With prices falling regularly you should have little trouble finding what you need.

## The extras

With CPU console, backing store and printer you have a very neat little general-purpose computer system. But there are many extra input and output peripherals you will want to add for specific purposes, or just for fun.

**Games controls**
These include attachments such as 'paddles' (racquets) and joysticks, controls which translate 'analogue' movements by your hands into digital information for the computer. Without something of this kind you have to use keyboard keys to move characters about in a game—one key for left, another for right, then down, sideways, and so on, plus one for a trigger button, to fire missiles or serve balls. It becomes tiring and confusing, and many games demand lightning responses. Joysticks give you greater freedom of movement, controlling all directions at once, and can also be of use for 'drawing' graphics accurately and neatly. Just coming onto the market is an interesting variant of the joystick, the **tracker ball**. This free-rolling sphere can be spun and twirled in its socket to send characters hurtling all over the screen with amazing speed and fluidity; at slower speeds it is much more accurate than a joystick. You can see these in use on full-size games machines such as **Missile Command**. However, they are still rather expensive.

**Graphics pads or digitisers**
These are rather the reverse of plotters; they allow

A typical joystick control, with a button to 'fire' guns, jets and so on

you to trace out an image in two dimensions straight into the computer's memory, converting the shape of the traced lines directly into digital information. The simplest ones work rather like pantographs, with joystick-type sensors in the arms.

**Keyboards**
One of the commonest concessions to price on a small computer is its keyboard. Many come with so-called 'touch' keyboards—better rechristened 'jab' or 'stub', as your fingers will agree. Compromise solutions such as the Spectrum's domed rubber sheet (affectionately known as 'dead flesh') are little better. You may want to add one of the many keyboards made for such machines by independent manufacturers. Number pads, like a calculator's keys, can sometimes be added; these are very useful if you take to entering machine code in a big way. Otherwise, all the keyboards presently available are standard typewriter layout, known as QWERTY from the first few letters; one wonders why, since this format was originally developed to **slow down** typists who were jamming early machines! Something like the hand-sized keyboard of the Microwriter word-processor could be a very useful alternative for home computers.

**Sound**
Extra outputs may also be useful. Most home computers now come with some kind of sound-generating facility, which you can use to provide sound effects for games or even to play music; as we saw in chapter 2, there are even programs to help you compose it. For machines that lack it, extension kits are often available, but these may cost more than a new machine would; for those with inadequate amplifiers and speakers, or only one 'voice', extension kits can generally be found. Check the advertisements, especially in user magazines for your make or model.

**Speech**
If you enjoy making people jump out of their skins, teach your computer to talk! Speech can be generated either by using a phonetic 'alphabet' which lets you program each word as a series of standardised sounds, or by a ROM chip containing very detailed instructions for generating a limited number of words. As you would expect, the ROM chip produces much more lifelike results, such as the newsreader's voice mentioned in chapter 2, but it can't say your name, or anything else particularly personal; it will reproduce program instructions and warnings very clearly, though. Phonetic speech comes out sludgy and mechanical, like a drunken Dalek (children love it!), and while it takes some practice to use well it can reproduce anything you want it to. There are simpler ways, too; you can buy software for some machines that acts like a graphics tablet for sound, turning any sound that is played into it from a recorder into digital information which you can—with practice—incorporate into your program. But this tends to produce rather approximate squawks. Simplest of all is to keep one track of the tape recorder for sound, as Atari and others do in addition to their own onboard sound facilities; speech is prerecorded and the tape activated as needed. If speech is important to you, check carefully; not every machine can handle it as yet.

**Monitors**
One of the selling points of home computers is that they will work on your own TV, but in fact this is not an ideal way. Your TV is designed to receive broadcast information, and the computer has to modulate its signal into this form via a video chip. It then outputs the signal along a cable to the TV's aerial socket, where it is received and demodulated into signals that drive the cathode-ray tube to produce the image. Every time the signal is modulated, interference and distortion are added. The result is often a rather wavery-looking image with 'creep' in the colours of the characters—indescribable till you've seen it, but hard on the eyes over any length of time. But the computer is quite capable of generating the signal in a form that will drive the tube much more directly; also, TV tubes and circuitry can be made more stable and efficient if they don't have to cope with broadcast conditions. Many computers, therefore, have

A sophisticated graphics pad in use on an Apple system

**monitor** outputs as well as TV ones. Monitors are, essentially, these superstable TVs, though some have tubes designed to resolve pictures made up of extra-large numbers of dots (pixels). One or two machines, notably the Sharp range, have monitors fitted as standard. They cost about the same as a good TV, but cannot generally be used as one without an additional tuner (if you can find one); monochrome monitors produce white, green or sometimes amber images on a black background, as a rule. Colour monitors produce the full colours of a TV picture. In both cases the result is much more like looking at a printed page than a TV, and much better for any kind of extended use, such as word-

For fine detail and sustained use, as here in word-processing, the clear, stable image of a monitor screen is a tremendous asset

processing. Ordinary TVs may soon be fitted with monitor-style facilities, as some video recorders are beginning to appear with monitor outputs also, but at present monitors have to be bought separately. They often have no sound facilities, which may be important, as many machines are beginning to use TV speakers to output theirs.

There are many more kinds of peripheral you can buy, or will soon be able to—control or speech-recognition facilities, perhaps—but this selection should keep you going for a while. No computer is an island, all to itself alone; without peripherals it is as handicapped as a human is without limbs. So don't think of the prices in the glossy adverts as all you'll ever have to pay; cost in peripheral prices, and you may change your mind as to what is and isn't a bargain in the long run. But on the other hand, don't think you **have** to have everything here; work out your needs, and choose your peripherals accordingly.

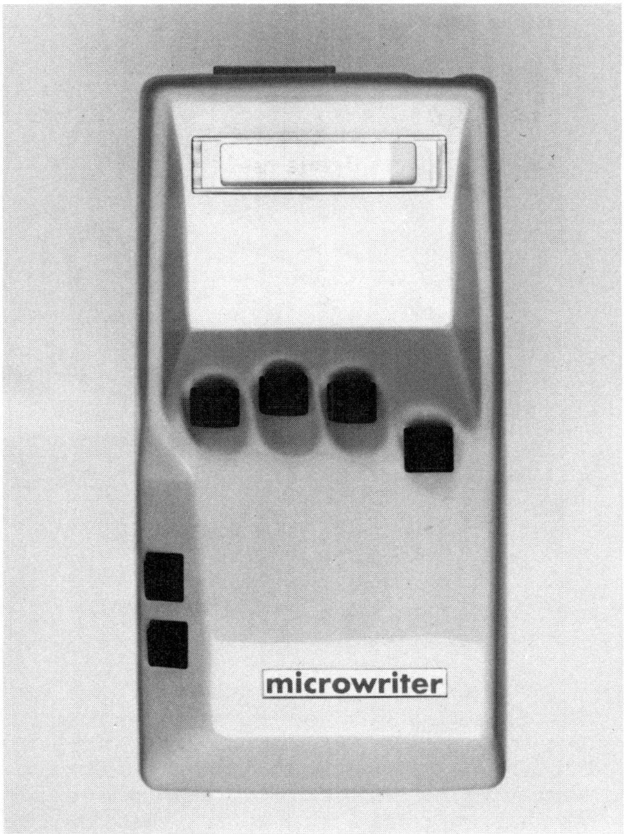


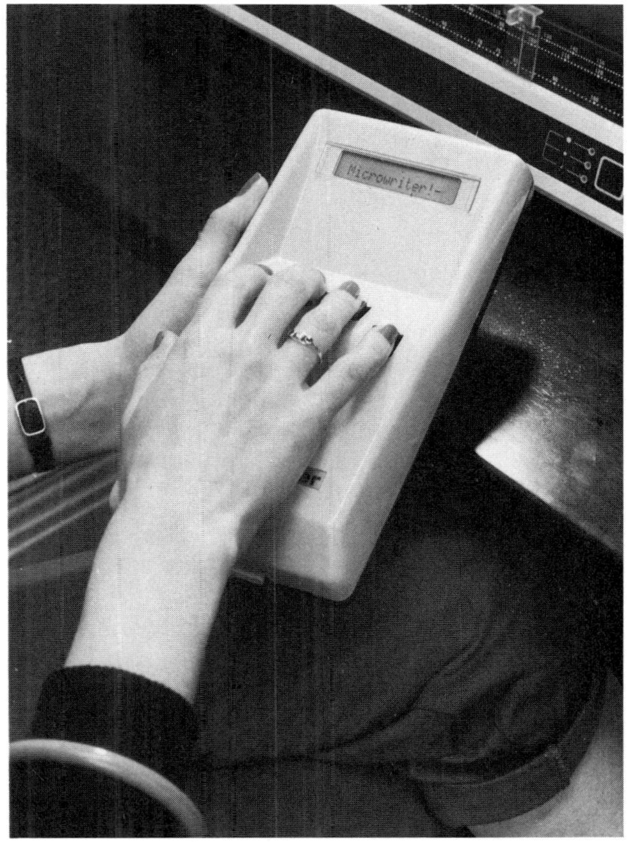


The remarkable Microwriter, a 'dedicated' word-processor invented by film director Cy Endfield. Unlike a normal keyboard, letters are not input by individual keys; instead the five upper keys, falling naturally under the fingers of the right hand, are pressed in patterns. You remember the patterns by diagrams relating them to the shape of the letter. It may sound complicated, but the record for learning to type with it is rumoured to be under two minutes! Unfortunately its high price keeps the Microwriter out of the normal home user's reach, but in the future a keyboard of this kind may make life easier for non-typists with micros

# 5. Which one do I buy?

By now, when you've seen just a little of what computers can do for you, and how, you may be wildly impatient to buy one for yourself. Don't be! Impatience is your worst enemy. Home computers are less expensive than they were, but still not exactly cheap; you can make some expensive mistakes, ending up with a machine that doesn't suit you and perhaps putting yourself off altogether. Impatience is the easiest way to do that. This chapter can't save you from every pitfall, but hopefully it will start you off properly, with a few useful tips. In the end, though, you will have to make up your own mind, and there is no better aid to doing that than actually seeing and trying out the machines that interest you most. Would you buy a car without a test-drive?

### Where do I start?

Here, with our survey of suitable machines later in the chapter. After that, in home-computer magazines (see chapter 7), and in a shop that stocks the machines you want—if you can find one. It may be a specialist computer shop, it may be a chain hi-fi or camera dealer, or even one of the large general stores like Boots or W.H. Smith. Don't expect too much from the sales staff, even—I almost wrote 'especially'—in specialist shops; listen to them, by all means, and ask as many questions as you like, but **don't** be sold something on the spot. Above all, watch the salesman who pushes one model in particular; it might be genuine enthusiasm, but it might also be that the machine is out-of-date, or overpriced, or pays him a better commission. Make it clear to him what **you** want to do with your computer, and ask him why that model comes closest to fitting your needs. Above all, get a demonstration; don't just settle for the salesman's quick once-over or the slick demonstration program—have a fiddle with it yourself, using the manual. (Assess the manual while you're about it—very important!) The salesman should let you do this, at least for the CPU console; novices are less likely to be let loose on disk drives or printers, where accidents could be pricey. If you are interested in a machine sold only by mail, don't despair; you will almost always find it on demonstration at computer shows and fairs (see chapter 7), though you may have to fight your way through a heap of bodies to get at it. A milder alternative, if it has been on the market for a few months, is to contact other users, perhaps through a user's group for that model (the manufacturers, or magazines, should help you find one).

### Which one's best?

The one that suits **you**. Home computers, like most things, are built more or less to a price. To reach it, manufacturers often economise—some say 'skimp'—on some facilities in favour of others. The result is that there is no universally 'best' machine with facilities enough to suit everyone; the ones that come closest to it are, naturally enough, often the most expensive. This makes your choice almost wholly personal. You must determine just what you want **your** computer to do for you, and how much you can afford to spend on it, and balance the two together against the machines available. Think of the things in chapter 2 that interested you most, and arrange them into some kind of order of priority. What will you want to do most and least? What at once, and what eventually? Remember that almost anything complex, or requiring extra equipment, such as word-processing or controlling model trains, will have to wait until you have mastered the CPU console and some programming, and can afford the extras. But above all, be honest with yourself. If you really just want to play games, don't persuade yourself that a business-oriented machine will be somehow more respectable to have; its games abilities may be limited, and you will have done yourself down. (And what's wrong with playing games, anyhow? They are essential exercises for the truly active mind and rich imagination. All the really intelligent people play them. I play them. So there!) Equally, if you are going to want a home machine mainly for business, scientific or mathematical uses, don't persuade yourself that a cheap games-oriented machine can cope. It can often be made to, and you might be surprised at how well; for example, there is a word-processing program which all but triumphs over the VIC-20's inadequacies. But the cost and inconvenience may surprise you even more. Whatever you want, why start at a disadvantage?

As a general guide, for the kinds of business and scientific application appropriate to small machines, you are likely to want substantial RAM capacity, readily available disk facilities, and a screen display in which clarity, the number of characters per line—preferably 80—and the ability to use a monitor are more important than colour. Scientific users may want high-resolution graphics, and business users modems and teletext facilities—a 40-by-25 character display option and a decoder. At the other extreme, a games user ought to have the best sound and colour graphics he can afford, along with joystick and perhaps ROM cartridge facilities. He can get by with a reasonable minimum of memory and his own TV for the moment.

However, there are many other factors which may influence your choice, especially if you have a clear idea of what you require, and we shall be looking at these next. But if you are fascinated by the possibilities of home computers and less sure of which ones you will eventually want—which is a perfectly reasonable way to feel—don't despair. Our survey of machines is divided up by price ranges, and in each range we have selected one machine whose overall spread of facilities and good value for money makes it, in our opinion, the best value for the uncommitted newcomer. But don't just take our word for it—look for yourself. Plenty of home computers are equally billed as having 'high-resolution graphics, 16K, colour and sound' but, as Orwell's farm animals swiftly found, some are more equal than others.

## Things to look out for

These are some of the main things you should be

Minutely sharp graphics created by a BBC micro. A high-quality display of this kind is always an asset, but for business or scientific applications it is little short of essential

looking out for, in any machine that interests you. They are not listed in any particular order; some are more important for particular uses, others are universally important. Without good servicing and support facilities you can be in deep trouble very soon, however superb the machine. You can find out the answers to the questions we ask from manufacturer's publicity (add grains of salt, to taste), magazine advertising (the same) and reviews, and from dealers. Absolutely nothing, though, should overrule the evidence of your own eyes; wherever and whenever you can, **see for yourself first**!

**Expansion**
How easy is this, if you'll need it? And how expensive? Can it be done directly, or must you buy expansion hardware? What ports (connections) does the machine have as standard? What expansions are available from the manufacturer? What expansions from other suppliers? How good are these, relatively? Must you use only dedicated equipment (as for the cassette deck), or can you use widely-available standard equipment?

**Software availability**
Is there a wide range of software available, both from the manufacturers and independent suppliers? (A sign of popularity more than actual quality, but encouraging; give new machines a chance, of course.) Most important, is there the software you want? From more than one supplier? How do they compare for price and quality? (Software reviews are becoming commoner in magazines.) What form does the software come in? What peripherals does it require? You should give some thought to all this even if you intend to write all your own programs. Even the best cooks eat out sometimes.

**Construction**
Is the case robust and inflexible? Does it overheat anywhere after the machine has been on for some time? (Most machines get warm, even those with external power units; look out for extremes.) How solid and secure are electrical connectors such as ports and switches? Is the keyboard, whatever the type, responsive and reliable? Check not only the reviews but the magazine problem-pages, and where possible user groups, to find out any common faults.

**Performance**
Is the microprocessor **significantly** fast or slow? (A lot depends on what you want to do with it.) Is anything else especially fast or slow—information transfer from cassette or disk, for example? Does this matter for your purposes?

**Languages**
As a newcomer you should start with BASIC. Is it supplied with the machine? If not, why not, and how much will it cost extra to get it? How is it supplied (in ROM, as a ROM cartridge, or in a form you have to feed in every time you switch on)? (The latter has **some** advantages, freeing more

A good range of input/output ports on the Commodore 64—joysticks and power input on the side, and ROM cartridge, TV, monitor, cassette, serial and expansion ports on the back

memory for non-BASIC software.) Is the BASIC dialect supplied flexible and easy to use? Does it have full facilities? Is it compatible with a standard BASIC such as Microsoft? 'Good' BASIC means different things to different people; Acorn's Atom BASIC is good for experienced programmers but thorny for beginners. Some BASICs supplied as standard are primitive but can be replaced or enhanced; is this possible? How much does it cost, and does it take up RAM space? And since you may want to move on to other languages eventually, are any supplied or available?

**Display and graphics**
Colour or monochrome? What resolutions are available? Does this include teletext-compatible mode? Does the display have both upper- and lower-case text as standard? (Essential for many applications, such as word-processing.) How easy are graphics to program? Are user-definable graphics available? Are sprite or player/missile graphics available? Can you mix text and graphics on the screen? If in colour, what range of colours? How many can be used at once in high-resolution modes? How good are the colours? (This varies enormously between computers and between TVs; arrange a home trial if you can.) How much RAM do high-resolution graphics leave free for the user?

**Sound**
How extensive is this facility? How many voices has it, over what ranges? How are they programmed? How easy is this? How is the sound produced—through an internal 'beeper' (piezo-electric speaker), a proper internal speaker, or through the sound systems of cassette or TV? Are pre-programmed sound effects available? Is speech synthesis available? Phonetically or stored-vocabulary chip?

**Keyboard**
For word-processing or almost any use involving much typing, anything less than a full typewriter-quality keyboard is guaranteed to drive you nuts. Is one fitted? If not, is one available, from the manufacturers or independent suppliers? Does the keyboard have extra keys for special user-determined functions, or can ordinary keys be taken over?

**Manuals and documentation**
I thought hi-fi documentation was the world's worst until I discovered computers. Early home-computer manuals were atrocious; among the worst was Commodore's **Pet** manual, and their track record is still not very good. Too many manuals are written almost as an afterthought, and by maniacal experts bursting with information they can't organise or communicate. Does the manual give you full, easy instructions on how to set up your machine, right from the word go? Does it lead you easily into a run-down and demonstration of the controls and facilities, or does it drop you right into a pile of heavy technicalities? Is there a proper BASIC course in it or with it? (Don't expect an exhaustive programming course.) Is it well provided with sample programs—not just demonstration efforts but one or two that actually **do** something? And is it clearly printed and well laid out, preferably with an index of BASIC commands and where to find them? A bad manual, though, needn't stop you buying a good computer (though by all means let the makers know what you think of it!); there are usually hosts of magazine articles and, for the more popular machines, books ready to fill in the gaps. A good start is crucial, and it's amazing how many manufacturers seem to have some trouble providing it.

**Dealer and manufacturer support**
And lack of it. Even the most helpful manufacturers tend to be rather remote creatures, accessible only after much writing and phoning, and few manufacturers **are** helpful; it hasn't dawned on many of them how strong a selling point customer relations can be. If you've bought by mail-order from them or an impersonal discount warehouse, you haven't much choice but to deal with them; however, it may be worth paying a little extra and buying from an established dealer. There should be at least one no further than the nearest large town; if you're stuck, ask the manufacturers. A good dealer will know all the ins and outs of the machines he sells, be able to give you good advice, demonstrations, and some swift problem-solving while you are learning to use the machine. He should be able to put you in touch with clubs and user groups (he may even be a member) and stock a good selection of software and books. Most of all, he should give you prompt service under guarantee, and a service contract when it expires. In all things he should act as an interface and not a buffer between you and the manufacturer. How do you find this paragon of dealers? Sorry, but I don't know a sure way, though club membership is usually a good sign.

If something does go wrong, though, even a mediocre dealer is someone you can get your claws into on the spot. In law **he** is responsible for the fitness of the goods he sells, and should give you a firm year's guarantee (at least). Some manufacturers still try to palm you off with 'limited' 90-day guarantees; these can't diminish your rights under the law. **Don't** sign any guarantee cards. If you are having trouble, and can't get any sense out of dealer and manufacturer, don't be too long-suffering; talk to any Citizen's Advice Bureau about your rights under consumer-protection laws. They will tell you more than I can here, but bear in mind the County Court Small Claims Procedure, which lets you take disputes over goods costing less than £500 to court without paying huge legal fees. To begin with, though, use the court as a threat—a lever rather than a club; point out that it'll cost them more, in time and trouble if nothing else, to fight the case than to sort out your problem!

**Unofficial support**

This covers all kinds of things—independent accessory and software manufacturers, user magazines, user groups and so on—that may exist around a particular model of computer. It even includes the grimly militant groups formed by those who ordered one **months** ago and haven't got it yet. This will all tell you something about the machine—first, that it is selling well, to support so much fringe activity. Second, the accessories on offer will give you some idea of what other users have missed most about the machine—the rash of cheaper and non-wobbly RAM expansions and proper keyboards for the ZX-81, for example; also, of which of the manufacturer's peripherals are overpriced—a conversion kit to let the VIC-20 use any cassette deck, for example. And third, as I have been stressing, a user's group is the best bridge between sales literature and the real world. Some users, though, get a little too religiously dedicated to the machine of their choice. Beware of these people. Insult their wives or kick their dogs if you dare, but **don't** knock their favourite computer! And try not to go that way yourself.

So with some idea of what you want from your first home computer, how you can get it, and how much you can afford to spend, you are ready to start looking. We have done our best to make things easier for you by including, over the next few pages, a survey of machines on the market that, in our opinion, are suitable for the first-time buyer. That doesn't mean they're in any way limited or restricted—quite the opposite. To us it meant, first and foremost, a price ceiling of about £400, the going rate for a decent video recorder; no first-time home user really needs to spend more. It also meant no machines that come in modular or kit form (except as an alternative); newcomers with little or no electronics experience can get themselves into terrible tangles with such machines, good as many are, and the saving is seldom large enough to justify the risk. We also left out so-called 'hand-held' or 'pocket computers'; again, many are good, but they are more like programmable calculators and so incapable of the same wide range of applications. Out also are one or two machines meant almost exclusively for educational use, without the broad software base of mass-market machines, and any survivors of the 'first generation' of home machines still on the market, such as the TRS-80 Model 1, Video Genie 1 and Commodore 4016. These machines have many virtues, not least the huge range of software available, but at their present prices they are living fossils offering the new home user less than he can get more cheaply elsewhere.

If any others are left out, it's because they weren't firmly enough on sale by our press date. Even so, we have included details of one or two 'hopefuls' that hadn't materialised as soon as they were meant to. Otherwise we have not been selective. We single out only what we think are the best all-rounders in each price bracket; remember, these aren't necessarily the best for the things that interest **you** most. That, alas, only you can decide; however, by 'characterising' these machines we hope at least to get you off to a good start.

The Video Genie I, a typical good first-generation machine that offered an inbuilt cassette deck, but only 16K RAM and no high-resolution graphics, colour or sound as standard at a relatively high price

**Database**

The price range divisions here are intended just as general guides, and are certainly not absolutes; prices change more or less constantly as new machines appear to compete, and more expensive doesn't necessarily mean better. We list the main facilities of interest to you for each machine—price (at press date), user memory, screen and sound facilities, keyboard type, languages supplied as standard (and in what form), main inputs and outputs, and the various expansions, peripherals and accessories available from the manufacturer (with a hint or two at non-standard ones). The comments that follow are meant to fill in a few gaps, but they are only opinions for you to take or leave as you like. Nobody's opinion, even that of the world's most knowledgeable reviewer, outweighs yours. You're going to have to live with the thing, after all.

**Under £100**
Still the bargain basement for home computers, and it is no accident that the best is also the most expensive.

**Coming attractions** **Binatone Colour Computer**—announced as having 16K memory (expandable to 64K), colour, sound, and a full typewriter keyboard, to cost around £50; rumoured to use similar chips to the Tandy Colour Computer and Dragon, so probably similar performance and software compatibility. At that price a bargain, but as manufactured in Far East and imported in bulk there is plenty of room for support problems. Check before buying!

**Commodore MAX**—pure games machine, with excellent graphics facilities of the Commodore 64, but only about 3K memory as standard and a plain touch keyboard. Expandable, but not recommended at around £100.

**Texas 99/2**—for about £80, 4K RAM, expandable to 36K, touch keyboard, no colour or sound; peripherals will include a colour printer and 50K floppy tape. Worth looking at.

**Creativision**—at £99.95, a close British competitor for Sinclair and Oric, with 16K RAM, four sound channels, high-resolution colour graphics, and a calculator-type keyboard. Interesting features include Microsoft BASIC and a range of dedicated peripherals—cassette deck, memory, interfaces etc.—which actually clip on to form a solid console.

**Texet TX8000**—another Hong-Kong Spectrum rival, at £98. With 8K RAM, text 32 × 16, graphics 128 × 64. Memory expansion module (to 64K) £52.

Price reductions may well bring the VIC-20, Spectrum 16K and possibly the Acorn Atom into this range; the best overall value recommendation remains unchanged.

**ORIC-1 (cheapest model)**

| | |
|---|---|
| PRICE<br>£99.95 | KEYBOARD<br>Touch (movable keys, but not full typewriter size); maximum 2 functions per key |
| USER MEMORY<br>16K (48K model available; no expansion advertised) | LANGUAGE SUPPLIED<br>BASIC in ROM |
| DISPLAY<br>Text: 28 × 40 (Teletext-compatible)<br>Graphics: High-resolution, 200 × 240<br>Colours: 8 | INPUTS & OUTPUTS<br>TV; monitor; cassette; printer (Centronics standard); external amplifier (hi-fi); expansion |
| SOUND<br>3 voices, 1 noise channel via internal speaker; pre-programmed effects for games | EXPANSIONS, PERIPHERALS & ACCESSORIES<br>Modem; printer and Microdisk drive to come |

COMMENTS On its overall specification, a remarkable little computer, and a powerful competitor even for more expensive machines. Other strong features include the ability to switch out BASIC when not needed, giving a full 64K RAM on larger models. A pity Oric's designers, the experienced microcomputer and Prestel-interface producers Tangerine, couldn't have managed a better keyboard; perhaps an independent supplier will produce one. For business users the cheap modem (£79.00 at press date) must be a considerable draw. Note, though, that early models have developed some irritating 'bugs' in BASIC and operating system. Like the Spectrum, the BBC micro and others, it has been launched too hastily. Little software as yet, but the manufacturers promise some.

## JUPITER ACE

| | |
|---|---|
| PRICE<br>£89.95 | KEYBOARD<br>Touchpad, rubber buttons; multi-function keys |
| USER MEMORY<br>3K, expandable to 16K (cartridge); language uses memory more efficiently than BASIC | LANGUAGE SUPPLIED<br>FORTH in ROM only |
| DISPLAY<br>Text: 24 × 32<br>Graphics: Low-resolution only, 64 × 46<br>Colours: monochrome only | INPUTS & OUTPUTS<br>TV; cassette; memory and other add-ons via two rear ports |
| SOUND<br>1 voice via internal piezo-electric 'beeper' | EXPANSIONS, PERIPHERALS & ACCESSORIES<br>Memory cartridge and printer interface announced |

COMMENTS The Ace looks a lot like an improved ZX-81, with better display (white on black), keyboard and sound (of a sort); hardly surprising, since it comes from ex-Sinclair designers. The case is very cheap and nasty. The real surprise is the language, FORTH instead of BASIC. FORTH is faster than BASIC, and immensely flexible; this makes it a good language to write your own games in. However, most people with no programming experience would find it harder to learn from scratch. But if you are already a seasoned programmer (on a school machine, or a friend's, perhaps) and don't mind a challenge, read a book or article on FORTH and consider the Ace. Remember, though, that the language is available at low cost for many other computers, and that since this is very much a programmer's machine there will probably never be much commercial software for it. Not, therefore, generally recommended.

## SINCLAIR ZX-81

| | |
|---|---|
| PRICE<br>£49.95 (Kit around £30) | KEYBOARD<br>Touchpad, with multi-function keys; single-key BASIC command entry |
| USER MEMORY<br>1K, expandable to 16K (cartridge); other manufacturers' expansions to 64K | LANGUAGE SUPPLIED<br>BASIC in ROM |
| DISPLAY<br>Text: 24 × 32, upper case only<br>Graphics: Low-resolution standard, 64 × 46; other manufacturers' high-resolution<br>Colours: Monochrome only | INPUTS & OUTPUTS<br>Cassette; TV; memory & other add-ons via rear port |
| SOUND<br>None | EXPANSIONS, PERIPHERALS & ACCESSORIES<br>16K RAM cartridge; thermal printer. Wide range from other manufacturers |

COMMENTS Really a first-generation machine, but its very low price makes it excellent value for a beginner **if** you are prepared to sacrifice some of the finer points, and therefore some enjoyment. In its favour is high level of support from independent suppliers of all kinds; enormous amount of software available, much of it rubbish (for games the **J. K. Greye** and **Quicksilva** ranges are often recommended). Not really for business, unless much revamped; probably cheaper to buy a superior machine in the first place. The keyboard is primitive and maddeningly complex.

## £100 - 200

Presently the area of hottest competition for the home market. Clear recommendation is harder than anywhere else, and hangs on fairly small points. Match **your** requirements all the more carefully.

**Coming attractions** **Acorn Electron**—a cut-down BBC micro, with slightly reduced graphics, 32K memory, and tape and TV ports only; others can be added as modules, at a price. At £150 this looks like a winner.

**Grandstand Computer**—about £160, from the Japanese firm Tomy but using a Texas 16-bit processor. With calculator keyboard, 16K RAM and high-quality graphics facilities—including good sprite graphics and sophisticated character-creation facilities—this is mostly a games machine, but a good one.

**Mattel Aquarius**—at £115.95, modular system from US toy and TV-game maker; 4K RAM, expandable to 52K in steps; high-resolution graphics, 320 × 192; 3 voices; touchpad keyboard; RS232 interface. Peripherals include dedicated cassette and printer; ROM cartridge software.

### COMMODORE VIC-20

| | |
|---|---|
| PRICE<br>£130 approx. from most sources (plus dedicated cassette recorder) | KEYBOARD<br>Full typewriter, with extra function keys |
| USER MEMORY<br>5K, expandable to 29K | LANGUAGE SUPPLIED<br>BASIC in ROM, expanded by cartridge |
| DISPLAY<br>Text: 23 × 22<br>Graphics: expandable to high-resolution 176 × 160<br>Colours: 8 | INPUTS & OUTPUTS<br>TV; cassette port (dedicated); cartridge and expansion port |
| SOUND<br>4 voices via internal and TV speaker | EXPANSIONS, PERIPHERALS & ACCESSORIES<br>Expansion box; joysticks; light pen; printer; disks. Some independent hardware |

COMMENTS One of the most popular machines on the market, but by no means an absolute bargain even if the price falls below £100; at present over-priced, given the very limited features it starts with, and the need to cost in a dedicated cassette deck. Expansion is not cheap, and is needed for some relatively simple functions. Keyboard and sound are excellent; display coarse, but a fairly wide range of software on cartridge and cassette makes the best of it. It is not impossible that the VIC-20 will go out of production in its present form soon.

## ACORN ATOM

**PRICE**
£174.50 (Kit £140)

**USER MEMORY**
2K, expandable to 12K internally, 32K externally

**DISPLAY**
Text: 32 × 16
Graphics: high-resolution in full version only, 256 × 192
Colours: monochrome standard; colour available

**SOUND**
Single voice, 'beeper'

**KEYBOARD**
Full typewriter style

**LANGUAGE SUPPLIED**
BASIC in ROM

**INPUTS & OUTPUTS**
TV; cassette; parallel port

**EXPANSIONS, PERIPHERALS & ACCESSORIES**
Memory; colour graphics, disk; printer; analogue/digital converter; also networking via ECONET system

**COMMENTS** The Atom is a good machine, but not for most beginners. It hovers uneasily between first- and second-generation machines; the extra facilities are there, but they push the price too high. The BASIC dialect is powerful, but far from standard and rather hard to handle. Compared with other machines there is little software available, though Acorn's own range is excellent; it includes semi-business facilities such as word-processing, though generally small-scale. The networking facility makes it a good school machine. At this price, though, there is better value, but the Atom has attracted many very loyal users.

## DRAGON 32

**PRICE**
£199

**USER MEMORY**
32K, expandable to 64K

**DISPLAY**
Text: 32 × 16
Graphics: High-resolution, 256 × 192
Colours: 9

**SOUND**
1 voice, via TV speaker

**KEYBOARD**
Full typewriter

**LANGUAGE SUPPLIED**
BASIC in ROM

**INPUTS & OUTPUTS**
TV; monitor; printer (Centronics standard); ROM cartridges; joysticks

**EXPANSIONS, PERIPHERALS & ACCESSORIES**
Expansion box (32K RAM, operating system and compiled BASIC) announced; disk controller and drive; joysticks; software ROM cartridges

**COMMENTS** An interesting machine, British-designed and made in Wales. Its strong points are obvious; its weakest points are probably its feeble sound and its graphics, generated by the same chip as the Tandy Colour Computer and just as limited. High-resolution mode allows only two colours—effectively, monochrome—and the quality, particularly on early models, is not that good; however, it does leave you 26K of user memory, far more than on many competitors. The BASIC, Extended Colour Microsoft, is about the best at this price, but the software is not; the manual is barely adequate. Will accept **some** Colour Computer cartridges, but none using BASIC—in different locations—or the C.C.'s serial port. Narrowly the best all-round value in this range, but outclassed by machines costing only a little more; popular, all the same, as it is sold through large stores, and its manufacturers have (so far) behaved responsibly.

## ORIC-1 (expanded model)

| | |
|---|---|
| PRICE<br>£169.95 | LANGUAGE SUPPLIED<br>BASIC in ROM; FORTH on cassette, free with 48K only |
| USER MEMORY<br>48K | INPUTS & OUTPUTS<br>as 16K |
| DISPLAY<br>as 16K | EXPANSIONS, PERIPHERALS & ACCESSORIES<br>as 16K |
| SOUND<br>as 16K | |
| KEYBOARD<br>as 16K | |

COMMENTS Even in this price range the Oric-1, with its full memory capacity, is a strong contender, keeping that slight edge over the Spectrum; however, it is now in competition with machines that have full keyboards and facilities such as disk immediately available. Consider it, nonetheless.

## SINCLAIR SPECTRUM (both models)

| | |
|---|---|
| PRICE<br>£125 and £175 | LANGUAGE SUPPLIED<br>BASIC in ROM |
| USER MEMORY<br>16K and 48K | INPUTS & OUTPUTS<br>TV; cassette; other add-ons via rear port |
| DISPLAY<br>Text: 24 × 32<br>Graphics: high-resolution 256 × 192<br>Colours: 8 | EXPANSIONS, PERIPHERALS & ACCESSORIES<br>Memory (internal, to 48K from 16K); Expansion module (RS232 interface; local network communications controller for up to 8 Microdrives); Microdrive (100K); Prestel interface |
| SOUND<br>1 voice via internal piezo-electric 'beeper' | |
| KEYBOARD<br>Touchpad, rubber dome keys on membrane; multi-function keys | |

COMMENTS Like the ZX-81, the Spectrum brought an enormous increase in computing power at a price the home user could afford, and made other manufacturers scuttle to compete. Excellent value both in itself and as the heart of a potentially powerful system; the promised peripherals have been a selling point from the word go. However, its production and reliability record over the first few months have been less than perfect. These, its poor sound and awkward keyboard (though better than some, including the ZX-81) lose it an overall recommendation.

## EG2000 COLOUR GENIE

| | |
|---|---|
| PRICE<br>£199.53 | LANGUAGE SUPPLIED<br>BASIC in ROM |
| USER MEMORY<br>16K, expandable to 32K | INPUTS & OUTPUTS<br>TV; monitor; cassette; RS232C (for modem); parallel port (Centronics optional); light pen; ROM cartridge |
| DISPLAY<br>Text: 40 × 24<br>Graphics: High-resolution, 160 × 96<br>Colours: 8 | EXPANSIONS, PERIPHERALS & ACCESSORIES<br>16K memory-expansion cartridge; cassette recorder (not dedicated); printer; Centronics printer interface and cable; joysticks; light pen |
| SOUND<br>3 voices, via TV speaker | |
| KEYBOARD<br>Full typewriter | |

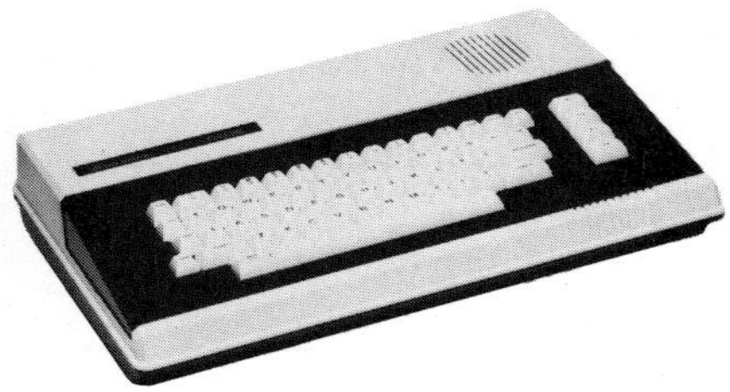

COMMENTS On paper this ought to have been the best value, even with its smaller memory capacity. In practice it looks a lot less attractive, although very well made and solid, and using a similar Microsoft BASIC to the Dragon's. However, Tandy software is **not** compatible. The graphics resolution is relatively low, and the graphics are pretty poor at any level, worse than the apparently related Tandy and Dragon versions. Sound facilities are good, and the multitude of I/O ports very impressive—except that too many of the peripherals you plug into them are over-priced to an extent that would be laughable if it were not so disappointing.

## SORD M-5

| | |
|---|---|
| PRICE<br>£189.95 | KEYBOARD<br>Touchpad, rubber dome keys on membrane; small multi-function keys; single-key BASIC keyword entry |
| USER MEMORY<br>4K RAM (expansion possible but not announced) | LANGUAGE SUPPLIED<br>BASIC in ROM cartridge |
| DISPLAY<br>Text: 40 × 24<br>Graphics: High-resolution up to 256 × 192; lower modes with larger character squares; sprite graphics facility<br>Colours: 8 + shades | INPUTS & OUTPUTS<br>TV; video; cassette; printer (Centronics standard); joysticks |
| SOUND<br>3 voices, via TV or video speaker | EXPANSIONS, PERIPHERALS & ACCESSORIES<br>paddle controls (supplied); software in ROM cartridge (2 games free) |

COMMENTS First appearance in the home market by a powerful Japanese business-computer manufacturer. Surprising, then, that this machine is only really suitable for games; the user memory is ridiculously inadequate and the keyboard is like the Spectrum's—'dead flesh' rubber keys with a confusing jumble of functions, here complicated by Japanese **kanji** (alphabetical) characters. However, against this there is a powerful 'spreadsheet'-style program available, and the monitor output may also count. But for the games user the graphics facilities—including sprites—are about the best available in this range, and the sound is also very good. Extra RAM could be added in cartridge form, as could some kind of disk or communications facilities, but there is no sign of either yet. Over-priced, but would not be overwhelmingly good value even at its Japanese price, £100. Available from Computer Games Ltd.

## TEXAS TI 99/4A

**PRICE**
£199 (£50 rebate scheme operated in 1982—price may fall after press date)

**USER MEMORY**
16K, expandable to 48K

**DISPLAY**
Text: 24 × 32
Graphics: High-resolution 256 × 192
Colours: 8 (plus 'Transparent', which lets one colour move behind another)

**SOUND**
3 voices, via internal speaker

**KEYBOARD**
Full typewriter

**LANGUAGE SUPPLIED**
BASIC in ROM

**INPUTS AND OUTPUTS**
TV; cassette; joystick; ROM cartridge; expansion port

**EXPANSIONS, PERIPHERALS & ACCESSORIES**
Expansion box (can contain any of following, sold seperately—32K memory expansion; up to 3 disk drives; Pascal language and interpreter; RS232 and other interfaces); disk drive; printer; speech synthesiser; ROM software

**COMMENTS** A good computer with a sad history of idiotic marketing; it was originally launched at high price, with an inadequate keyboard and unconverted to the European PAL TV system—you had to pay for an American NTSC monitor too! These faults have been corrected, but it has rather missed the boat; despite being centred on an early 16-bit microprocessor it is beginning to look a little out-of-date. The BASIC in particular is inadequate; the **Extended BASIC** cartridge is needed almost from the word go. But the TI 99/4A is well designed and built, the graphics are good, and the software, though expensive, is generally quite good and wide-ranging, with some serious business potential. Sound and speech are excellent. At its rebated price of £149, the Texas would be the best all-round value in this range; even at £199 it is worth considering.

**£200 - 300**
Here sound back-up and support are at war with theoretically superior facilities. Bear in mind that it's more tolerable to pay for upgrading than repairs—or even to find you can't get them done. Software availability is also a more powerful element in your choice than before. If the price of the Commodore 64 fell into this range it would be a clear overall recommendation.

## ATARI 400

**PRICE**
£199.95 (plus BASIC cartridge and dedicated cassette deck)

**USER MEMORY**
16K, officially unexpandable (but see below)

**DISPLAY**
Text: as 800
Graphics: as 800
Colours: as 800

**SOUND**
as 800

**KEYBOARD**
Touchpad, single membrane with no separate keys

**LANGUAGE SUPPLIED**
None (BASIC in ROM cartridge available)

**INPUTS & OUTPUTS**
as 800, without monitor

**EXPANSIONS, PERIPHERALS & ACCESSORIES**
as 800

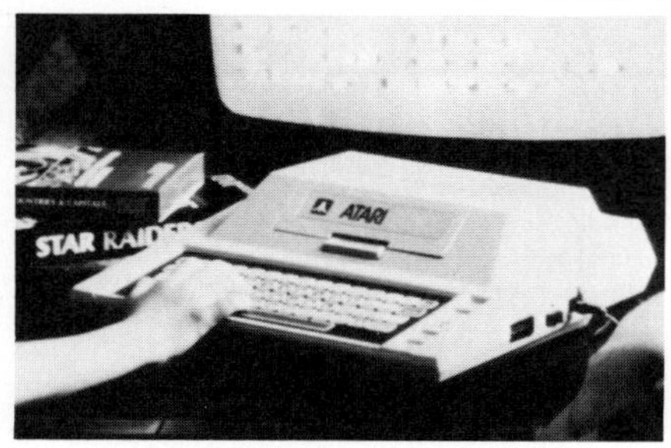


**COMMENTS** Atari tried to sneak this under the magic £200 limit by leaving out the BASIC cartridge, but without it all you've got is a TV game. And as you also have to buy their cassette deck, at a price, I feel it belongs on this side of the limit. But even here it is quite good value if you don't want to do a lot of typing; the keyboard is discouraging. The memory isn't large, but British dealers market upgrades right to the 48K maximum; Atari discourage these only because they make the 800 worse value, but the price of them does shoot the 400 into the next price range. So does the proper keyboard from the same sources. If you do opt for these, make sure your dealer will match the voided Atari guarantee. In this range the MPF-II, with an equally nasty keyboard but no expensive cassette deck, is probably better value, but Atari support is likely to be much better.

*At press date Atari cut the price to £159.99 plus £39.95 for the BASIC cartridge. The 400 is now 6p under £200—however, there is still the cassette deck.

## BBC MICROCOMPUTER MODEL A

| | |
|---|---|
| PRICE<br>£299 | KEYBOARD<br>Full typewriter, with extra function keys |
| USER MEMORY<br>16K, expandable to 32K | LANGUAGE SUPPLIED<br>BASIC in ROM |
| DISPLAY<br>Text: up to 40 × 25 (Teletext compatible)<br>Graphics: High-resolution, up to 320 × 256 (increases with expansion)<br>Colours: 8 + shades | INPUTS & OUTPUTS<br>TV; B/W monitor; cassette |
| SOUND<br>3 voices via internal speaker | EXPANSIONS, PERIPHERALS & ACCESSORIES<br>Upgrade kit (memory & I/O facilities) to model B; otherwise as for model B |

COMMENTS A cut-down version of a very good machine indeed, but not particularly good value in itself because the superb graphics are RAM-hungry, and can leave you with very little memory for the rest of a program. There are other annoying limitations, such as the I/O facilities. In sum, the only reason for buying a model A is to upgrade to a model B as soon as possible, and you should think twice about that because the upgrade usually costs substantially more than the £100 price difference. **Don't** be taken in by super-cheap '32K memory expansions'; they generally don't give you the extra I/O facilities included in the official upgrade, such as analogue/digital ports for joysticks.

## TANDY TRS-80 COLOUR COMPUTER

| | |
|---|---|
| PRICE<br>£233 | LANGUAGE SUPPLIED<br>BASIC in ROM (Extended Basic on expanded models or upgradable) |
| USER MEMORY<br>16K, expandable to 32K | INPUTS & OUTPUTS<br>TV; cassette; RS232; 2 joysticks; cartridge & expansion port |
| DISPLAY<br>Text: 32 × 16<br>Graphics: High-resolution, 256 × 192<br>Colours: 8 | EXPANSIONS, PERIPHERALS & ACCESSORIES<br>Memory; various printers; plotter; disk drive and controller; speech synthesiser; Extended BASIC in ROM; wide range of ROM cartridge software |
| SOUND<br>1 voice, via TV speaker | |
| KEYBOARD<br>Typewriter format, large calculator keys | |

COMMENTS As with many US imports, the Colour Computer has always been rather overpriced, to an extent which not even good documentation and support could make up for. Apart from the rather second-rate keyboard, it is not a bad machine, but it is in direct competition with its close relation, the Dragon; a Tandy with Dragon specification—32K, Extended BASIC—costs no less than £469 at full price and £379 at the more usual 'reduced' rate. And the Dragon has a proper keyboard. Tandy software is better than anything I have seen from Dragon, and their documentation is really impressive; I have found their shops friendly and helpful. But the price is still a stumbling block.

## LYNX

| | |
|---|---|
| PRICE<br>£225 | KEYBOARD<br>Full typewriter |
| USER MEMORY<br>48K, expandable to 192K (in switchable blocks) | LANGUAGE SUPPLIED<br>BASIC in ROM |
| DISPLAY<br>Text: 40 × 14<br>Graphics: 512 × 248 (expanded version)<br>Colours: 8 | INPUTS & OUTPUTS<br>TV; monitor; RS232C; cassette; Centronics optional |
| SOUND<br>1 voice, via internal speaker | EXPANSIONS, PERIPHERALS & ACCESSORIES<br>Memory, disk drive with controller announced |

COMMENTS An interesting computer from a very small company (Camputers Ltd.), with almost ideal specifications for a home machine and a strong small business potential. Graphics are excellent, sound is feeble, and software, at press date, is non-existent; the BASIC, a dialect written specially for the Lynx, is a strange mixture of strengths and weaknesses; an expanded version is promised. Despite the tempting specifications of the Lynx, it is hard to recommend it as a first-time buy when it is in this embryonic state and its future depends so much on its market share, and on the software that becomes available. Certainly delays in its launch did not get it off to a good start.

## MPF-II (MICROPROFESSOR)

| | |
|---|---|
| PRICE<br>£270 | LANGUAGE SUPPLIED<br>BASIC in ROM |
| USER MEMORY<br>32K (out of 64K, not expandable) | INPUTS & OUTPUTS<br>TV; monitor; cassette; printer (Centronics standard); ROM cartridge port; add-on port; external amplifier |
| DISPLAY<br>Text: 40 × 24<br>Graphics: High-resolution, 280 × 192<br>Colours: 6 (at all resolutions) | EXPANSIONS, PERIPHERALS & ACCESSORIES<br>Chinese character generator; printer; speech & extended sound generator; RS232C; disk drive and controller; ROM language and other software cartridges; remote-control box; keyboard |
| SOUND<br>1 voice via internal speaker | |
| KEYBOARD<br>Small calculator keys; single-key BASIC entry optional | |

COMMENTS There is one trick about this machine its specifications don't reveal; its BASIC and electronics are compatible with those of the Apple, the most popular US home computer (though the MPF-II is not, like some less reputable efforts, a slavish copy). Since the Apple has probably the best and widest software range of any home computer, but is grossly overpriced for the British home user, this is tempting. But most Apple software comes on disk, so you must also cost in disk drives, which are not yet available. Even so, this machine would have been an outright choice, with its excellent graphics, if it had only had a better keyboard; at press date an add-on was announced—at extra cost, of course. There is also the serious question of service and support that hangs over any machine imported by a company other than its manufacturers. Despite that and its lack of further expansion, well worth a look if the keyboard doesn't put you off.

## NEWBRAIN Model A and AD

| | |
|---|---|
| PRICE<br>£269.95 | LANGUAGE SUPPLIED<br>BASIC in ROM |
| USER MEMORY<br>32K, expandable to 2 Mb (in switchable blocks) | INPUTS & OUTPUTS<br>TV; monitor; cassette; printer (RS232/V24); communications (RS232/V24); expansion port (for expansion module) |
| DISPLAY<br>Text: 40 × 30 or 80 × 30 plus built-in 16-character display on model AD only<br>Graphics: High-resolution 256 × 250 to 640 × 250 (depending on expansion)<br>Colours: monochrome only | EXPANSIONS, PERIPHERALS & ACCESSORIES<br>Expansion module (memory-switching circuitry; parallel ports; analogue/digital ports; V2 ports; ROM expansion space); memory modules; networking modules; disk control modules; battery backup pack; teletext module; printers, monitors, disk drives and hard disk announced; software in ROM |
| SOUND<br>None | |
| KEYBOARD<br>Typewriter style, small keys | |

COMMENTS In its AD form this is the only truly portable computer in our survey, able to run on batteries and output to its onboard screen, and that is now its greatest strength. Although it first appeared on the market in 1982, it was announced two years earlier by another company, and is really an advanced first-generation design. As such, although its graphics are quite good, its lack of colour and sound facilities make it less generally interesting to home users, and its marketing is aimed quite squarely at business, educational and scientific users. But if you really want a machine that can be used normally and as a portable, this is presently the cheapest; however, it may soon be overtaken by others, perhaps including Sinclair.

**£300 - 400**
At these heights the air is already getting a little thin for home users. You have a right to expect both superior entertainment facilities and at least some serious business potential; consider peripheral prices carefully, as they're often jacked up in this range, on the principle that it looks less expensive relative to the CPU.

## ATARI 800

| | |
|---|---|
| PRICE<br>£399.99 (plus dedicated cassette deck) | KEYBOARD<br>Full typewriter |
| USER MEMORY<br>48K | LANGUAGE SUPPLIED<br>BASIC in ROM cartridge |
| DISPLAY<br>Text: variable up to 40 × 24<br>Graphics: High-resolution, variable between 12 × 20 and 320 × 192; player/missile (sprite) facilities available<br>Colours: 8 + shades | INPUTS & OUTPUTS<br>TV; monitor; cassette (dedicated); serial port (Centronics/RS232 optional via interface module); 4 joysticks |
| SOUND<br>4 voices, via internal speaker and TV | EXPANSIONS, PERIPHERALS & ACCESSORIES<br>Dedicated cassette deck; printer; interface module; disk drive; joysticks and paddles; large range of software in ROM cartridges, cassettes and disks |

COMMENTS

Really the Rolls-Royce of home computers, with all the advantages and disadvantages that name suggests. Everything is designed for user convenience; even the operating system and RAM come on plug-in cartridges, easy to change or add to. Sound is good and graphics superb (not too RAM-hungry, either). BASIC a little basic but acceptable (a version of Microsoft Colour BASIC is available, but not on ROM). The other software is slickly powerful, and very well documented (not so the computer; you will need a book like **De Re Atari** to get the best out of it), and **Star Raiders** is the computer game everyone raves about. Business potential is also good, with a good word-processing program and much else. So what's the drawback? **Price.** Everything about the Atari costs a fortune, and not all of it—the printer, for example—can possibly live up to it. And the differences between the 400 and 800 are not really enough to justify the huge price differential (which was a full hundred pounds greater until late 1982). Software in particular is pricey—though no worse than video game cartridges. So, buy the Atari by all means—but be prepared to spend more quite soon.

## BBC MICROCOMPUTER MODEL B

| | |
|---|---|
| PRICE<br>£399 | LANGUAGE SUPPLIED<br>BASIC in ROM |
| USER MEMORY<br>32K | INPUTS & OUTPUTS<br>TV; 2 monitor; cassette; RS423 (RS232 compatible); Centronics; user port; 4 joysticks; Tube (second processor facility); optional ROM-cartridge socket |
| DISPLAY<br>Text: up to 80 × 30 (inc. Teletext compatible mode)<br>Graphics: High-resolution, up to 640 × 256 (monitor quality)<br>Colours: 8 + shades | EXPANSIONS, PERIPHERALS & ACCESSORIES<br>Monitor; printer; joysticks; modem announced; disks announced; Econet networking interface; voice synthesiser and other ROM chips |
| SOUND<br>3 voices via internal speaker | |
| KEYBOARD<br>Full typewriter, with extra function keys | |

COMMENTS

An Acorn design refined to meet exacting BBC requirements, this is a remarkable machine in almost every way. Its launch was disastrous, as I have mentioned elsewhere, but it should remain readily available now; buy from stock rather than by mail-order if you can, though (always a good idea anyway). Its main flaw is lack of memory; at full strength the graphics eat about 20K (which is why the model A can't produce them!). But they **are** superb, the sound is good and the BASIC excellent (and generally Microsoft compatible). It loses out to the Atari in general ease of use, and amount and quality of software available—though what there is is cheaper, and Acorn's own Acornsoft range approaches Atari quality. On earlier models the operating system was dodgy: find a new one if you can, or be prepared to **pay** for a replacement chip! That probably accounted for occasional program-loading problems from cassettes; if you run into this, a 'patch' routine is available to help. Choice of cassette deck may also affect this, but at least you **can** choose. That is the final factor—no dedicated cassette—that makes the BBC Micro the best value in this range.

## COMMODORE 64

| | |
|---|---|
| PRICE<br>£340 (plus dedicated cassette) | LANGUAGE SUPPLIED<br>BASIC in ROM, expanded by cartridge |
| USER MEMORY<br>38K (58K if BASIC interpreter switched out) | INPUTS & OUTPUTS<br>TV; monitor; cassette (dedicated) serial port; ROM cartridge port; 2 joystick ports; user port (optional RS232); second processor facility |
| DISPLAY<br>Text: 40 × 25 (Teletext compatible)<br>Graphics: High-resolution, 320 × 200; sprite graphics facility<br>Colours: 8 + shades | EXPANSIONS, PERIPHERALS & ACCESSORIES<br>Cassette deck (as VIC); printer (as VIC); disk drive and controller (as VIC); modem announced; joysticks; ROM cartridges for Extended BASIC, networking, etc. (Will run MAX games cartridges **but not VIC**). |
| SOUND<br>3 voices, via TV or hi-fi | |
| KEYBOARD<br>Full typewriter; extra function keys | |

COMMENTS A wolf in VIC's clothing, because outwardly it differs only in colour and badge. The BASIC is also the same, unfortunately, a rather primitive dialect dating back to the famous PET. This makes it very hard to use the excellent graphics. Extended BASIC makes up for this, but gobbles up all that excellent memory (and costs £50 extra!) The sound is superb, with the range (nine octaves) and capability of a small synthesiser. There is also plenty for business users, including just about the best word-processing package on any home computer at press date. Since VIC cartridges are unfortunately not usable, there was little software at press date. This and the BASIC are its main drawbacks in comparison with the other machines in this range; its price could fall, though, in which case it would become better value in this range or the best in the £200 - £300 league.

**Over £400**

Frankly, I am inclined to feel that this is more than most home users should spend on their first machine in its most basic form. There's nothing puritanical about this—it's simply that you tend to run into the law of diminishing returns. Until you move up into a much higher price bracket, you don't get that much extra for the extra money, at least not in things that make a great deal of difference to home users; the improvements tend to be specialisations in some particular direction—usually business or educational—and often make the machine less interesting in other ways. Colour and sound may not be fitted as standard, or even available, and good games software may not be available either. The extra money might be better spent upgrading a cheaper basic machine—adding interfaces to the Atari 800, for example—or adding peripherals such as disk drives. But there are one or two rather more expensive machines that are worth a look at if they happen to suit your particular needs.

For around £550 (or as little as £500 if you shop around) you can buy the Sharp MZ80A (not to be confused with its predecessor the MZ80K, similar but with an impossible keyboard, or with the more expensive MZ80B). The price is high, but for it you get essentially a complete unit, a 48K computer with keyboard, cassette deck **and** black-and-white monitor screen in one case. Unusually, the ROM only holds minimal operating and screen software; the BASIC comes on cassette and has to be 'booted' into RAM before use. This has the advantage of leaving the full amount free for other software if you don't want BASIC, and only takes a minute or two to load. There is only a limited sound facility and, obviously, no colour; peripherals are good but very expensive, and there is a reasonable range of software, both games and business. It is likely to interest semi-business users most.

Sharp MZ80A

The same goes for the Epson HX-20, but for very different reasons. This is another self-contained system, but in miniature—in fact, it is only an inch or two larger than this book, and about two inches deep. That space contains a full typewriter keyboard, a microcassette drive for data storage, a little impact printer, a small liquid-crystal screen (like a larger digital watch or calculator) and a sophisticated computer with BASIC in ROM and 16K memory, expandable to 32K. All this, plus rechargeable batteries that will run it for up to 50 hours. A TV/monitor adaptor and other peripherals such as full-size printers and disk drives can be added, and a range of software is announced—so far only business programs, which seems appropriate. For around £460 (plus another £75 for the microcassette drive, which can be interchanged with extra memory modules) this is remarkable value; the little screen is a slight handicap, but acts as if it were a window onto a much larger screen—an effect like reading text through a magnifying glass, a small segment at a time. Wholly unsuitable for games, the HX-20 is perfect for a small-business user who needs to move about a lot; it can be used quite comfortably resting on your knees. All in all, a beautiful little machine.

Lastly, a machine announced in America but not yet available elsewhere. This is the Atari 1200, which appears to be essentially an upgraded 800 with an increased memory capacity; it can now offer up to 56K RAM and a neater case, but it is hard to see what other advantages there are to justify the extra price (probably around £500). However, it may become clearer when more details are available, so if the Atari range attracts you, keep your eyes open.

## Buying second-hand

Frankly, I don't recommend this. A lot can go wrong with a computer that doesn't show up at once, even during a thorough test; some faults related to overheating take an hour or two to appear, but once they're there, they stay. There's less of a problem if the machine is still within its guarantee period—but in that case, why is it being sold so soon? The owner may have discovered it isn't quite as entrancing as it looked. More significantly, though, you seldom save a great deal by buying second-hand; most people who sell want to upgrade to another, pricier, machine, and can't afford to drop the price much. Also, very often the shop price has fallen since they bought, making their price look relatively higher. If you are buying second-hand from a reputable dealer he should give you some sort of guarantee (three months, perhaps) but since this ups the cost a little and he has to add V.A.T. you are even less likely to get a bargain. If you're offered a gift horse, in fact, you **should** look it in the mouth; has the manufacturer or importer gone bankrupt (making service harder to get)? Has this model some appalling design flaw? Is it wildly out-of-date? Probably the best way to buy is from an experienced friend who is ready to help you get to know the machine before asking you to make up your mind, and hopefully has some software and peripherals he is ready to sell with it. Generally the best second-hand value seems to be in first-generation home machines such as the TRS-80 Model 1 and Commodore Pet series—**if** you can tolerate limited memory, low-resolution graphics, no sound and monochrome display. Some of these deficiencies can be rectified, of course—at a price, which may absorb the initial saving. Their main advantage is the enormous range of software which has been built up over the years.

## Timing

Finally, never worry if you can't afford the one and only computer that will do just what you want. Progress in electronics is so fast these days, and competition between manufacturers so fierce, that if you're prepared to wait a little there is a very good chance that either the machine of your dreams will drop in price or some other manufacturer—quite often Clive Sinclair—will bring out something similar but radically cheaper. It **might** even be better. Looking through magazines of only a year ago can be like ancient history! Between November 1981 and November 1982, for example, the shop price of one popular machine fell by nearly a third, as rival machines hit the market. Between June and December 1982 another nose-dived from about £600 to about £400. You might think that kind of thing couldn't go on for ever; maybe not, but even allowing for research and development costs, most manufacturer's profit margins still leave them plenty of room for manoeuvre.

Of course, if you followed this attitude to its illogical conclusion you would never buy, because there'd always be something better just around the next corner. It just pays to pick your buying time carefully. If a splendid new machine does appear, take your time about buying that, too. All too often manufacturers seem to treat the launch of a new machine as a chance for some final development work financed by the customers. So the machines appear with horrifying faults which the eager buyers run head-first into. Eventually, of course, the manufacturer will correct these, with much mopping and mowing and expressions of deep regret, mostly directed at his next lot of customers—'...but we **have** corrected this on all machines made since September ...' One manufacturer who launched his machine with a barely adequate but dodgy component had the gall to charge early customers a 'nominal' £10 for replacing it! So join the later customers, and let the fools rush in ahead of you if they want to.

This applies especially to machines sold by mail-order only. In 1982 the Sinclair Spectrum and the Acorn BBC micro were launched this way, promising delivery within 28 days. People flocked to send in their money, but apart from review models, the computers themselves were very slow to appear. Over the next few months an increasing tide of complaints brought nothing but soothing blandishments and apologies, citing 'huge demand' as the main problem, and promising rapid delivery 'in the next few weeks'. Acorn ceased to advertise; Sinclair did not, and went on promising 28-day delivery. It was later admitted that in fact there were deeper problems with both machines; the entire Spectrum circuit board had to be redesigned. Few people waited less than three months for their machines; I have heard of some waiting eight or more. Others demanded refunds, were promised them, and had to wait almost as long. Sinclair sent effusive apologies and a small free gift; Acorn, as far as I know, sent nothing.

Both machines, let it be said, are everything they were supposed to be. Both companies pleaded for understanding. But it is not the customer's business to be understanding, especially not when he has parted with money that could have been earning interest for him; where was it during these delays? Without any deliberate attempt to deceive customers you cannot call what happened fraudulent, but to me at least it seems scandalously irresponsible. You should draw your own conclusions from this. By all means order by mail, but be sure that delivery is promised within 28 days; if it doesn't come, inquire once, then contact the Consumer Council, the Advertising Standards Association, and the magazine or paper that carried the advertisement. You are quite justified in complaining.

# 6. How do I make it work?

POKE it? That might not sound like the best way to get off on a friendly footing with your new computer, but it's done in the best circles. In fact, POKE is a command in the computer language called BASIC—one of the more advanced commands, in fact, and one which gets you on the most intimate terms with your machine. It does this by combining two related but very different methods—machine code and high-level language—of giving the machine the sequence of orders and information on which it operates—its program. You make your computer work by programming it, and that's what this chapter is all about. It won't take you as far as using POKE, unfortunately, because like many commands—such as those for sound and graphics—its use differs from machine to machine. The commands we will be using are common to most machines, and the programs are short enough to follow on the page.

## Computer languages

We have already encountered these, but we should now take a closer look at them, and how they are used.

### Machine code

As we saw in chapter 3, the microprocessor takes in and puts out information in the form of the binary code it understands, its particular **machine code.** Machine code is therefore the most direct way of programming a computer; coded information occupies only the necessary minimum of memory addresses and needs no translation to be processed. Programs written in machine code make the most economical use of RAM and run through more quickly; you can therefore do more with machine code, and do it faster.

Unfortunately machine code is very hard for the beginner to use in all but the simplest operations. You have to translate the entire series of operations into code form, step by minute step; entering great masses of numbers is slow, it's difficult to keep track of what you are doing, and one tiny error can turn the whole program into gibberish. Even experienced programmers find it slow going, and so very early in the history of modern computers they began working in a numerical system based neither on 2 nor 10 but on 16—**hexadecimal** or **hex** for short. Hex looks a little weird to non-mathematicians because our standard Arabic numbers only go up to 9 in one column; for one-column equivalents of 10 to 15, therefore, hex borrows A to F from the alphabet. One hex number represents half an 8-bit binary number; to translate it you need only use a table, or, better still, feed a very brief program to the computer first which will recognise hex numbers you feed in and generate their binary equivalents—acting, in other words, as a kind of translator.

**Decimal, hexadecimal and binary equivalents**

| decimal (base 10) | 'hex' (base 16) | binary (base 2) |
|---|---|---|
| 0 | 0 | 0000 |
| 1 | 1 | 0001 |
| 2 | 2 | 0010 |
| 3 | 3 | 0011 |
| 4 | 4 | 0100 |
| 5 | 5 | 0101 |
| 6 | 6 | 0110 |
| 7 | 7 | 0111 |
| 8 | 8 | 1000 |
| 9 | 9 | 1001 |
| 10 | A | 1010 |
| 11 | B | 1011 |
| 12 | C | 1100 |
| 13 | D | 1101 |
| 14 | E | 1110 |
| 15 | F | 1111 |

16 was chosen as a base because with 4 bits—half a byte—you can define up to 16 numbers

### Low-level languages

Though easier to work with, hex programs are still wholly numerical, and so nearly as hard for most people to follow. But when you are using a translation program that already has to recognise letters and output their binary equivalents, it isn't too hard to take it a stage further and use little groups of letters to represent the instruction part of the program. These **acronyms** (NATO and SALT are acronyms) can be made to indicate what they actually do—STA for the command 'Store a number', for example. So, suddenly, instead of communicating with the computer by numbers alone, you are 'speaking' to it in something that has some faint resemblance to human language, and even to English, and it is suddenly much easier to follow the sequence of operations in a program, because each instruction has a clear meaning at a glance. When you feed in the sequence of acronym instructions and numbers, the translation program 'assembles' them into a machine-code program, which you can then run; the translator is therefore known as an 'assembler', and the acronym system it handles as an 'assembly language'.

**High-level languages**

Assembly-language programs, though, still have to spell out every single step the computer has to take; in other words they follow the computer's way of 'thinking', and not a human's. For that reason they are still rather heavy going to work in, though still comparatively fast and economical. As memory space became cheaper, though, and more people needed to write programs quickly and simply, they developed symbolic instruction systems which tended to follow human logic rather than the computer's. Instead of following each individual operation of the computer, they grouped these into preset sequences that added up to simple actions, represented by appropriate code-words; the translation programs recognised these and generated not one but a whole sequence of instructions. The programmer no longer needed to specify such things as memory addresses, or each separate step of processes such as multiplication; the code-word generated all the necessary actions.

The translation program had to be much more complex, of course, but there were fringe benefits; low-level languages, because they follow the

How do I make it work?

Among the many high-level programming aids available for most machines are programs which simplify or extend the use of their graphics facilities. This rich 'Persian Carpet' design was created on a BBC micro with Acornsoft's **Creative Graphics** program

computer's actions so closely, are less likely to run on a different machine. But with a high-level language relying on standardised code-words, you should only need to change the translation program. Things haven't worked out quite that easily, unfortunately, because computer manufacturers seem to like nothing better than inventing their own versions—'dialects'—of a theoretically standard language, and frantically proclaiming their dialect's superiority to every other kind. There are few, if any, signs of sanity in this direction.

At present there aren't as many dialects as there are machines—there are more! Manufacturers persistently equip their machines with their own versions of BASIC, however outdated and idiosyncratic. As a result they or independent manufacturers have to bring out an expanded version of BASIC—usually expensive and memory-hungry—or a whole new version. This is usually close to the excellent BASIC developed by the US firm Microsoft; this, particularly in its Extended Colour form, is as near a standard as anyone gets at the moment. But, judged by the number of users, the most popular dialect is Sinclair BASIC; as it is also very clear to follow, it is used in our program examples later in this chapter.

**Compiler versus Interpreter**

Originally, high-level languages were translated in much the same way as low-level ones; the translation program—the **compiler**—was fed into the computer and the actual program was then fed in as information to be processed. Out came a machine-code program ready for use. Programming was a desk job; you sent your program to the computer, and only found the mistakes—'bugs'—in it when you got back the results. At the time people were still using clumsy methods like punched cards or paper tape to communicate with the computer, and it was only worth using these in long sequences. But the development of the Visual Display Unit—combining television and typewriter keyboard—made it easy to get information in and out more directly and in small amounts. A different kind of translation program then became popular, one to which the program could be fed a step at a time, and even checked for commands which didn't make sense; the translator could then send back an error message, perhaps even identifying the kind of mistake. This kind of program is known as an **interpreter**. Many enthusiasts still prefer compilers, as compiled programs are faster and more economical, but interpreters are infinitely easier to use; they are fitted as standard on almost all home machines.

**Popular languages**

A number of high-level languages were developed in the late 1950s and early 1960s, the best-known being FORTRAN (FORmula TRANslation Language), ALGOL (ALGOrithmic Language) and COBOL (COmmon Business-Oriented Language). COBOL's main use is self-evident, ALGOL is primarily scientific and mathematical, and FORTRAN is used for both. All of them, though, were and are rather diffcult for newcomers to computing to understand and use, and so in the 1960s a new language was developed for students at Dartmouth College, N.Y., USA; it was called Beginners' All-purpose Symbolic Instruction Code—BASIC. Actually, the name does it less than justice. It has far outstripped its originator's intentions, becoming much more than a teaching language; its relative clarity and great flexibility make it the ideal small-computer language, and it is the standard language supplied with every home computer except one.

Error messages vary widely from interpreter to interpreter, some being rather inscrutable—like this; others come as codes you have to look up in the manual, but the best ones politely spell out exactly what's gone wrong

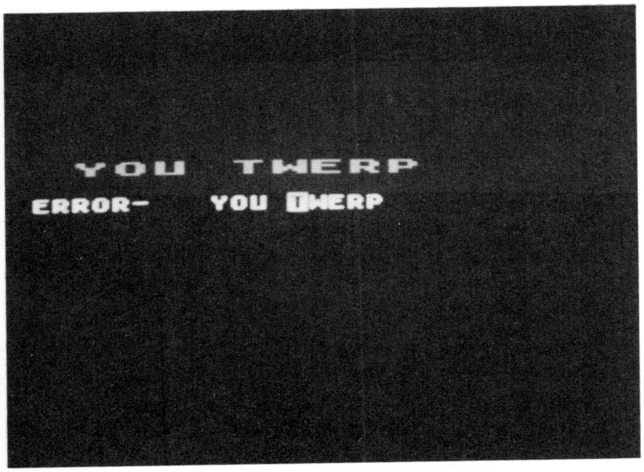


The exception uses FORTH, the latest and perhaps most likely in a series of rivals to BASIC. BASIC is much sneered at by many professionals, and most of all by academic computer experts, who dislike what they call the sloppy programming it makes possible. There is a grain of truth in this. In BASIC you don't have to define the actual processes in a program minutely; you can do things the long and rambling way round, and they will work—after a fashion. You can get to John O'Groats via Lands End—after a fashion. But try it too often and you are likely to cure yourself of the habit. I mention this because so much magazine ink is wasted running down BASIC in favour of languages such as APL, PASCAL (last year's fashion) and FORTH (this year's fashion), that you might develop an inferiority complex about using it. Don't. Fashions change, but BASIC sails blithely on as a good general-purpose language and at present the **only** one to start with. Later on, when you have mastered it, you can certainly try your hand at some of the more exotic languages; PASCAL is a faster, more complex cousin of BASIC, and FORTH is a rather weird and cryptic language, very fast and good for games—compiled, not interpreted—but hard for anyone except the program's author to make sense of. However, you might first like to try machine code via an assembler, laborious as it is, because that is the way to milk the last ounce of performance out of a small machine.

But it may be that all high-level languages, and not just BASIC, will soon lose out to even higher things. Some programs are available which practically take over parts of the programming process. Among these are so-called 'spreadsheet' programs such as Visi-Calc, largely for business and financial planning, which will automatically adjust all areas of a plan when one is altered; for that they are sometimes called 'what-if?' programs. Even more radical are the new generation of programs spearheaded by the challengingly-named **The Last One**—billed as the last program you will ever need to buy. This is because it and its rivals actually generate programs, in response not to line-by-line instructions but a more general outline of the task—something not unlike the flowcharts we will encounter later in this chapter.

Theoretically these ought to have thrown every programmer out of work the day they went on sale, but of course they didn't. The problems and solutions involved still have to be analysed and defined up to the flowchart stage, and that is perhaps the greater part of programming skill. And even after that, individually-written programs are usually just that little bit better; tailor-made clothes fit better than off-the-peg. But these program generators do work; at the moment they are mainly business-orientated, but it cannot be long before something similar is developed for the home user. Imagine, for example, being able to create a household-expenses program tailored in great detail to your own circumstances and special problems through one of these programs, or having one that took the background, rules and graphics of a game you had thought up and did the hard work of actually bringing it to life? In fact, programming aids like these are already beginning to appear; many home computers on the market have what are called 'sprite' or 'player/missile' graphics facilities. These are 'objects' which you can easily shape and move around the screen—say, as space monsters and the missiles that shoot them down—very easily in any game you want to invent. If writing your own games is important to you, then choose a computer that offers them. Critics might claim you were losing all the machine's intellectual value that way, and bringing it closer to being just a toy or houshold gadget. I don't agree. People who want to learn **will** learn, however 'user-friendly' computers are made; have cars that are easier to drive created more or fewer mechanics? And why should we restrict the advantages of driving to those few people who have the skill—and the time—to design a good differential system?

## Programming

For the moment, though, you are going to have to know at least a little about programming to get the maximum enjoyment out of your computer. But you won't learn it here, or in any other general book about home computers—no matter what it claims. You could write a whole book this length about programming and still have many more bookfuls to say.

So why cover the subject at all? As with the rest of this book, to give you an idea what to expect. Far too often programming has become wrapped in special mystery, sometimes by business programmers out to baffle their bosses, sometimes

A simple flowchart for getting up in the morning (see page 79)

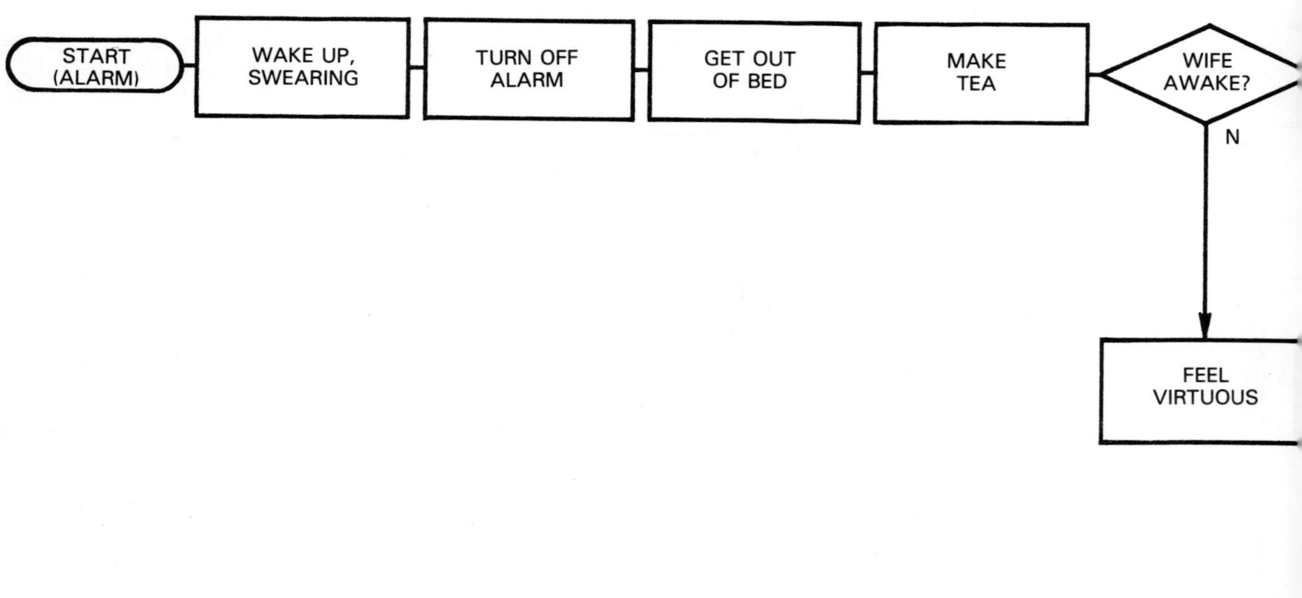

by the cloistered attitudes of many computer scientists and academics. Some have genuine trouble making things clear to outsiders, while others—a sad minority, I hope—actually enjoy playing the High Priest, guardian of knowledge forbidden to lesser mortals. Don't let them grind you down—it's their egos that need attention, not yours.

But if you are going to invest in an expensive home computer, it's as well to have some idea of how to program it, even if you don't intend to do anything very ambitious yourself. So now we are going to take a very brief look at how a problem can become a program, and at how some of the main commands in BASIC are used to create such a program.

**The problems**

The human mind is a wondrously complicated thing. All the time it is performing really complex feats of logic and reasoning, but we tend not to notice these because they have become such a habit. Look out of the window and see if it looks like rain. It takes you no mental effort at all to come up with one of three main answers—'Yes,' 'No,' and 'Actually, it **is** raining!'. But in fact you've been carrying out a whole series of fantastically detailed observations: in effect, asking yourself a series of questions and basing decisions on the answers—is the sun shining? Are there clouds about? If so, are they solid or sparse, grey or white, heavy or fluffy? Does the horizon look dark? Are there little flecks of water on the glass? And so on. You can analyse the situation outside that window at a glance, because your brain knows just what questions to ask and what calculations to make with the answers—**if the sun's shining and there are no clouds, it probably won't rain for a while,** or **if the sky's grey with cloud and the horizon looks dark, there could be rain about.** Experience and acquired knowledge have taught your brain a sequence of actions to carry out to solve the problem you have set it. You could call that sequence a program.

Computers, though, can't learn from experience—not without another program to tell them how. So you have to break down every problem you set a computer into a series of actions—acquiring information, calculating on the basis of that information, and making a decision based on the result. Sometimes the breakdown is pretty obvious, as when you want the computer to add 2 and 2 (though remember you must tell it to give you the result!). But most of the time it isn't, and before writing a program you must analyse the problem behind it. One of the easiest ways of doing this is a

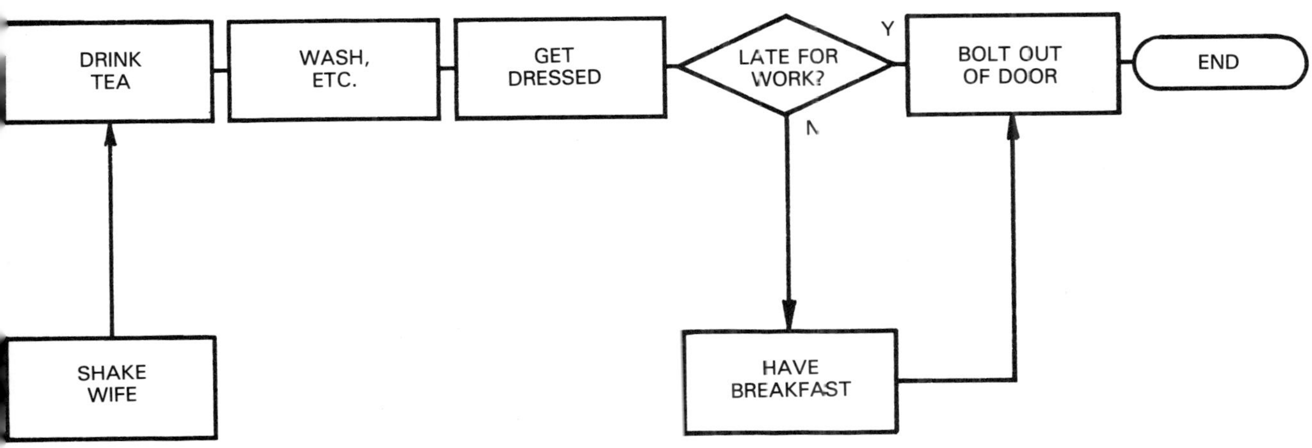

Making tea

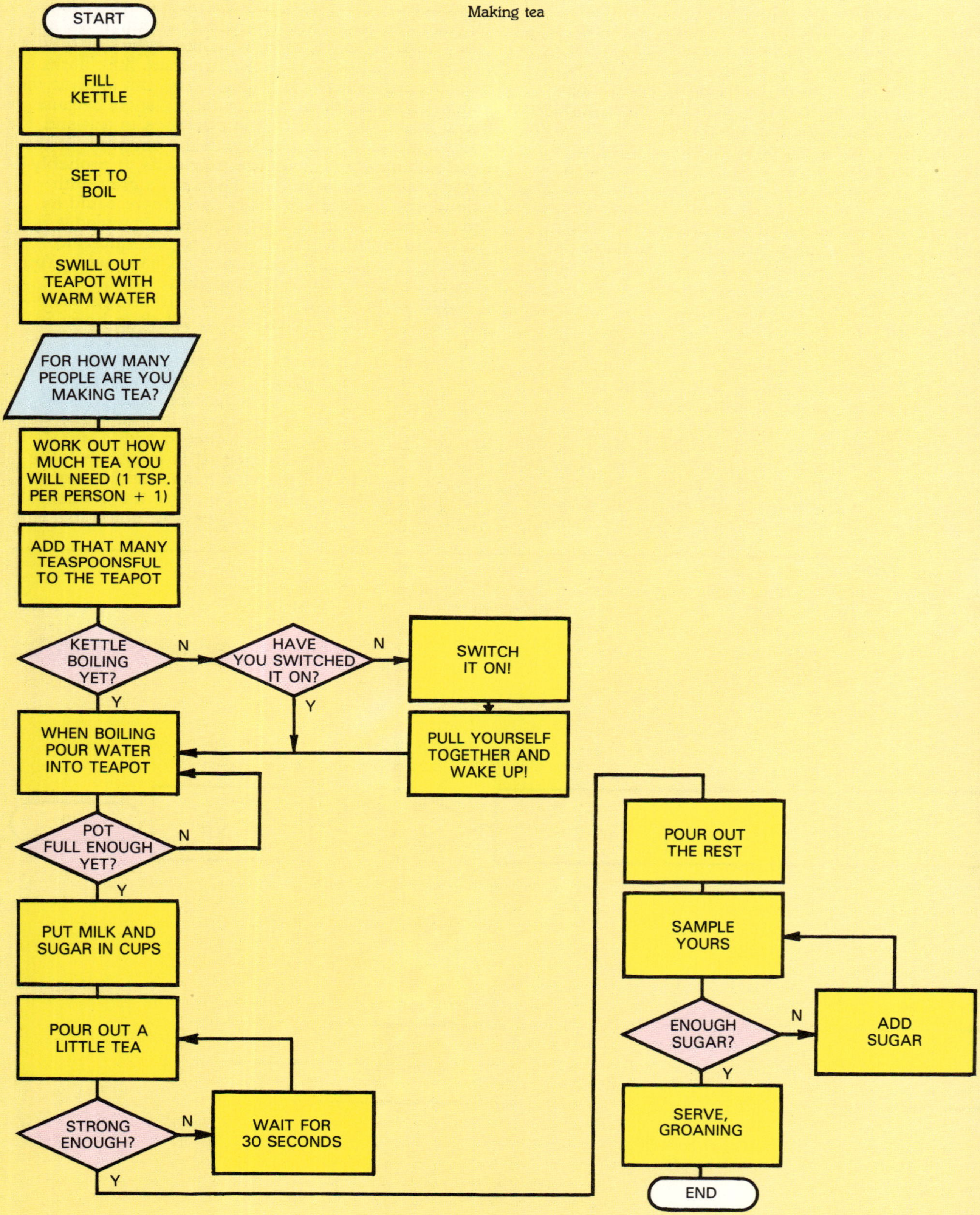
START
FILL KETTLE
SET TO BOIL
SWILL OUT TEAPOT WITH WARM WATER
FOR HOW MANY PEOPLE ARE YOU MAKING TEA?
WORK OUT HOW MUCH TEA YOU WILL NEED (1 TSP. PER PERSON + 1)
ADD THAT MANY TEASPOONSFUL TO THE TEAPOT
KETTLE BOILING YET?
N
HAVE YOU SWITCHED IT ON?
N
SWITCH IT ON!
Y
Y
PULL YOURSELF TOGETHER AND WAKE UP!
WHEN BOILING POUR WATER INTO TEAPOT
POT FULL ENOUGH YET?
N
Y
PUT MILK AND SUGAR IN CUPS
POUR OUT A LITTLE TEA
STRONG ENOUGH?
N
WAIT FOR 30 SECONDS
Y
POUR OUT THE REST
SAMPLE YOURS
ENOUGH SUGAR?
N
ADD SUGAR
Y
SERVE, GROANING
END

diagram known as a flowchart.

You can turn almost any process into a flowchart, and in a variety of levels of detail. On pages 76 and 77 is a simple chart for getting up in the morning. But any part of that flowchart could be broken down into a much longer chart—the tea-making stage, for example (see page 78).

Take a look back at the box in which you decided how many spoonfuls of tea to use. Suppose you wanted to make a chart showing how to make tea for any number of people, not just two. You would then have to express the link between the number of people and the number of extra spoonfuls; the best way to do this is algebraically—for **x** people use **x** extra spoonfuls. So the total number of spoonfuls to use will be **x** + 1. However, you couldn't just go on adding more spoonfuls for more people indefinitely, or the pot would overflow; it can only hold so much tea, up to a maximum limit. So your chart will have to say '**x** + 1 spoonfuls up to an upper limit of—' What? However much the pot will hold. But you should allow for different pots, too, so you have to set the upper limit as another algebraic symbol—**y**. Such symbols are called **variables**, for obvious reasons. You set this at the beginning of your chart, and when the tea-making formula comes round you simply say 'add **x** + 1 spoonfuls up to a maximum of **y**. If **x** + 1 is greater than **y** you need another or a larger teapot.' You now have a very useful formula. Read in another way, it could be used to estimate just how large a teapot, or how many, you would need to make tea for **x** people; you could add an upper limit to mark when a tea-urn would

Does it look like rain? If you ever feel the need to have your computer decide for you, why not illustrate your program? With good graphics (here the BBC micro) you could even animate the clouds, or change their colour to suit the weather

become necessary. In effect, you have isolated the core of the problem of how to make tea and turned it into a mathematical (or logical—much the same) relationship which remains constant even when the figures change. And in doing that you have taken your first step in programming.

Not a very useful one, though, until they bring out a home computer with robot arms to handle the pot and temperature-sensing gear for the water, etc. Meanwhile an ordinary teamaker will do the job well enough. For our first look at an actual BASIC program we will want to choose something a little more sensible, a program you can actually bring to life on your machine when you buy one. However, we have to use one that is simple enough for you to follow by yourself from the page, without benefit of computer. That, alas, rules out a lot of interesting games programs because they tend to be long, and sometimes use graphics commands, which vary widely between versions of BASIC and are hard to bring to life from the program listing alone. So we will choose something short and useful enough to please any Victorian philosopher.

Suppose you are moving to a new house, and you need to work out its floor area to calculate the cost of new carpets. We will work through a number of versions of a program to help you do this, and in the process see some of the commonest BASIC commands at work. Remember, in every case, that the command word may have relatively little relation to what it actually does, just as the drill sergeant's 'Atten-**shun**!' is not an order to become interested but to assume a stiffly upright stance, and his 'Stand at—ease!' means 'Assume one of the least easy postures ever invented!'

### Carpetbag program

So it is with our first command, PRINT, which dates from the days when teleprinters were the most efficient way of communicating with the computer. It actually does three things; it will perform a calculation and put it up on the screen, it will put up on the screen the contents of a variable such as **x**, or just 'print' out anything in inverted commas. So the simplest way of using your computer to calculate these floor areas is to measure the length and breadth of the first room—say, 5 metres long by 7 metres wide—and type in PRINT 5 * 7. (Computers sensibly use an asterisk as a multiplication sign because it can't be confused with x, the letter.)

The answer, 35, will come up on your screen. You do the same with the rest and tot them up. Not very impressive so far, but then you are still at the one-off stage, tea for two. Isolate the core of the problem and use variables. Whatever the size of the room, you will need to multiply length by breadth —x * y. But you can't just PRINT x * y; you need some way of getting the various values into the variables. You could use two commands to set the values, turning the single instruction into a set of three stages. In BASIC each stage is numbered, for both your and the computer's convenience. So you type in:

```
10 LET x=5
20 LET y=7
30 PRINT x*y
```

You number each line in tens to leave plenty of room to insert extra lines as afterthoughts; these you will always have, and most often when you haven't left enough room for them! Now you have written your first program; to activate it, type in a RUN command, and the answer 35 will again appear. But for your next room you will need to type the whole program in again—back with tea for two. You want something to insert the new value each time; this is the INPUT command. And while you're about it, why not add some text to remind you just what to put in, and in what order? For that you use PRINT in its other meaning:

```
10 PRINT "Type in the room's l
ength:"
20 INPUT x
30 PRINT "Type in the room's b
readth:"
40 INPUT y
50 PRINT "The area is:"
60 PRINT x*y
70 PRINT "square metres."
```

RUN this and type in values 5 and 7 when the screen asks you to, and the result will look like this:

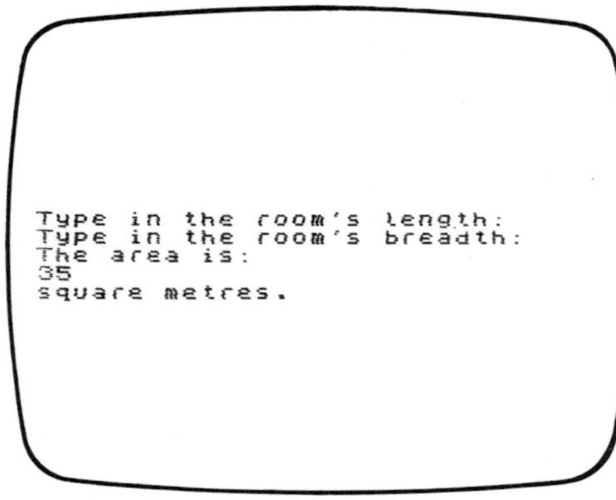


Fine, so far. But you still have to add up each room's area yourself. What you want now is a way of running through that sequence as many times as you have rooms to carpet, collecting the totals as you go and adding them up. This you can do with some extra variables—a,b,c—and just two new commands. Very important ones, though; IF...THEN embodies the computer's power to discriminate and to make decisions. It does this by deciding whether something is equal to (=) something else, not equal to it (< >), less than it (<) or greater (>); the last two signs can be used with = to indicate **less than or equal to** (<=), or **greater than or equal to** (>=). We are going to use one of these compound forms now. Pretend you are the computer and follow our revised program through to see what it does:

```
    2 PRINT "We have six rooms to
  carpet."
    5 LET b=0
    7 LET c=1
   10 PRINT "Type in the room's l
 ength:"
   20 INPUT x
   30 PRINT "Type in the room's b
 readth:"
   40 INPUT y
   50 PRINT "The area is:"
   55 LET a=x*y
   60 PRINT a
   65 LET b=b+a
   70 PRINT "square metres. The t
 otal so far is:"
   80 PRINT b
   90 PRINT "square metres."
  100 LET c=c+1
  110 IF c<7 THEN GO TO 10
  120 PRINT "That's all, folks!"
```

(note the inserted line numbers)

(b will hold the increasing total)

(This line will be the first half of our looping system; see lines 100, 110)

(The first line altered. Since a now holds x times y, we can just print it instead.)

(This increases the total.)

(The count is upped by 1.)

(The computer checks if the count is finished. If not, it goes back.)

The second new command is GOTO or GO TO, always referring to a line number. It can be used on its own or following IF...THEN (some BASIC dialects have an IF...THEN...ELSE... command). Here it creates a loop in the program, controlled by c, the counting variable; every time a room area is calculated, line 100 adds another 1 to its value till it reaches the preset limit. Then because c has exceeded this the computer goes on to line 120 for the first time. Incidentally, this program touches on two of the commonest mistakes budding programmers make—either forgetting to empty variables when no longer required, or emptying them by mistake. If line 110 had ended '...GOTO 2' or 5 or 7 it would have emptied the total variable and the counting variable c, setting them at their original values. This time we do not need to empty variables x or y because a completely new value is input each time—but watch out when creating loops of this kind!

Our program now works, but in a rather long and roundabout way. There is a neater way of managing a repeating program, using one command less.

Replace line 7 with:

7 FOR c = 1 TO 6 STEP 1 (STEP 1 means 'count intervals of 1'; intervals can be any size.)

And line 100 with:

100 NEXT c

And throw away line 110 altogether. This rather cryptic little sequence uses the counting variable c in just the same way as before, but more neatly; also, it doesn't refer to a line number, so you can alter the program more freely. Now you can rewrite the program a little to incorporate this, and while you're about it produce a more sensible screen display. The changes are fairly radical, so you might as well take the chance to renumber the lines in intervals of ten again.

```
   10 PRINT "You have six rooms t
 o carpet."
   20 LET b=0
   30 FOR c=1 TO 6 STEP 1
   40 PRINT "Please enter the roo
 m's"
   50 PRINT "A) Length:","B) Brea
 dth:": INPUT x,y
   60 CLS
   70 LET a=x*y: PRINT "The room
 area is ";a;" square metres."
   80 LET b=b+a: PRINT "Total so
 far is ";b;" square metres."
   90 NEXT c
  100 PRINT "That's all, folks!"
```

Yes, you can put more than one command on a line in most kinds of BASIC, but it's better not to do so too indiscriminately; it tends to confuse the logical sequence and makes it harder to adjust. You might end up wasting what space you save elsewhere. Here, though, it tidies up the display—with very careful punctuation. In BASIC the punctuation signs are also commands, arranging the sequence of actions in a line. As we have seen, quotation marks mean that nothing contained in them is BASIC; it's just text to be printed back out. So in line 50 the colons inside quotation marks are ignored, while the one immediately outside tells the computer to move on to the next command. Semi-colons in lines 70 and 80 run a line of actions together under PRINT. A comma acts like a set tabulator control on a typewriter, shifting the next action halfway across the screen. So in this program you will first get a screen looking like this:

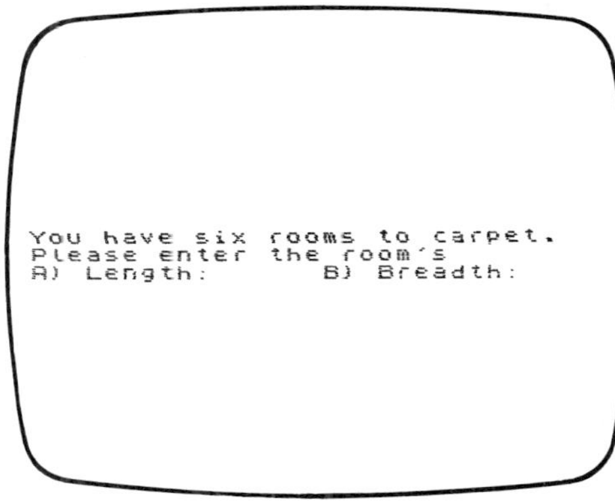

As you type the figures in, they will appear under the appropriate headings, until you press 'ENTER'. But then line 60 comes into play. The CLS command stands for 'clear the screen', and it does this. The words disappear and are replaced by:

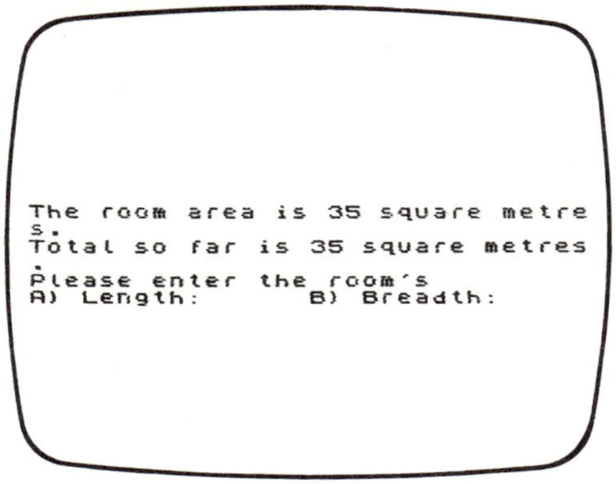


It will continue to display the size of the last room entered, the total so far and a request for the next set of measurements, until the total is reached; line 100 then finishes it off instead.

So far, so good. But our program still only tackles a part of the problem. What we really want to know is how much those carpets are actually going to cost, and we can work that out from the overall area only if every room's carpets are going to cost the same amount per square metre. If so, we can just add a couple of lines to input the cost and multiply it by b. But in practice this will seldom be the case. It would be much better if we could calculate the price for each individual room and total that up. For that, though, just setting a room total won't really be enough; we need to identify each room as it is covered, and list it at the end. Then we can have an open-ended program that simply loops as often as you ask it to. A rough flowchart for it is given in the next column.

Not too difficult to make up out of the commands we already know, is it? Except for the matter of names. To handle those we need to use a new kind of variable, a **string variable**. The ordinary variables we have used so far can only hold numbers, but a string variable can hold any kind of character or mixture of characters. It is defined by the $ sign, and holds its data between inverted commas; so, to set it at nothing you enter LET x$ = "". When you start studying BASIC in earnest, you will find that strings can be used in all kinds of ways. One simple use is to have the computer call its user by name, in just the way it names the room in the program below; it is easy, too, to booby-trap a string so that when it receives a given name—say, "Fred"—it immediately replaces "Fred" with a hair-raising insult. Everyone else it treats normally...

In this more complex program, it may help us to distinguish between ordinary and string variables. Many, though not all, BASIC dialects will let you label variables with full names, not just letters—

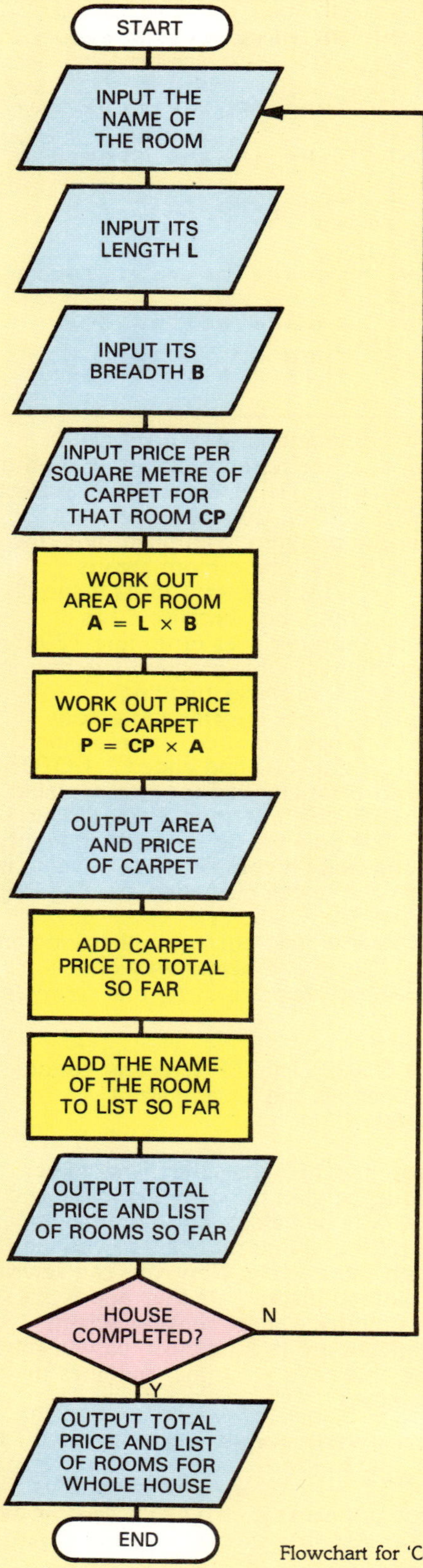


Flowchart for 'Carpetbag' program

though this uses a little more memory, of course—and we have taken advantage of this to identify the ordinary variables clearly. Also, the program begins with a REM command; this stands for 'remark', and tells the computer to ignore the contents of that line because they are simply a label or note put in for the programmer's use. In this case it contains the program's title, or file-name, which is used when loading it into backup storage such as cassette or disk.

```
   5 REM Carpetbag
  10 LET l$=""
  20 LET Totalprice=0
  30 PRINT "Enter the name of a
room:"
  40 INPUT r$
  50 CLS
  60 PRINT "Enter the ";r$;"'s l
ength (metres)": INPUT Length: P
RINT Length: PRINT "and Breadth:
": INPUT Breadth: PRINT Breadth
  70 PRINT "and the price per sq
uare metre (in pounds) of the ca
rpet you would like?": INPUT Pri
ce: PRINT Price
  75 REM Price in pounds (adapta
ble to any decimal currency you
like)
  80 CLS
  90 LET Area=Length*Breadth: LE
T Roomprice=Area*Price
 100 PRINT "Thank you. In that c
ase the cost of carpeting your "
;r$;", which is ";Area;" square
metres in area,"
 110 PRINT "will be £";Roomprice
;".": PAUSE 100: CLS
 120 LET Totalprice=Totalprice+R
oomprice: PRINT "The total cost
of carpets so far is £";Totalpri
ce
 130 LET l$=l$+(r$+", ")
 140 PRINT "Rooms so far covered
: ";l$
 150 PRINT "Are there any more r
ooms to quote for? (yes or no, p
lease!)": INPUT a$
 160 IF a$="yes" THEN GO TO 30
 170 CLS : PRINT "So, carpets fo
r your"
 180 PRINT l$
 190 PRINT "are going to cost yo
u £";Totalprice;"."
 200 PRINT "That's all, folks!"
 205 STOP
```

If you enter 'bedroom' at the beginning, r$ will go on printing out 'bedroom' in its place in all the sentences, until a new meaning replaces it when the program repeats. The variable l$, set to nothing in line 10, is there to provide an accumulating list of the rooms you have so far covered. It does this by adding on the current contents of r$, plus a comma and a space for neatness' sake, in line 130. Like algebraic brackets, BASIC brackets 'contain' a calculation, so that only its result comes out and is acted upon by anything beyond the brackets. Remember that the computer cannot, like us, see a whole line at once; it has to work methodically along it, character by character. The third string, a$, contains the answer to the question in line 150; the IF...THEN command compares the input meaning with a fixed value, just as it did for numerical strings. An answer for 'no' could have been included, but why bother? Answer anything but **yes** and the computer will automatically move onto the next line, by default. But using the same technique you could extend a question and answer routine like this to cope with all kinds of contingency, and provide the illusion that the machine is carrying on a conversation. It isn't; you are, at one remove.

Like its predecessors, the Carpetbag program is really very short—necessarily so, to make it easy to follow. It would hardly tax the memory of even the smallest computers in our lists, so you will get some idea of what you could do with the larger ones. When you get one of your own you will soon see ways a program of this kind could be extended—it could cope with paint and wallpaper as well, for example, or even furniture in relation to floor area. It could easily be made to draw diagrams of something like that. Related problems—the area of oddly shaped rooms, say—could be handled by subsidiary programs called subroutines; these are attached as extra line numbers after the end of the main program, and reached by the command GOSUB, plus the subroutine's first line number. The command RETURN in its last line takes you back to the main program at the line after the GOSUB command. This is especially useful when you have to carry out the same type of operation—relating cost to area, say—several times in the course of a program. Instead of typing in each separate calculation, you just refer it to a subroutine. By tacking it onto an IF...THEN command, GOSUB can also be used for operations that aren't needed every time—calculating the cost of underlay, for example, only when the carpet needs it.

There are more possibilities for this, or any other program you dream up for yourself, than I can

Computers calculate your phone bill—why not write your own program to keep track of it?

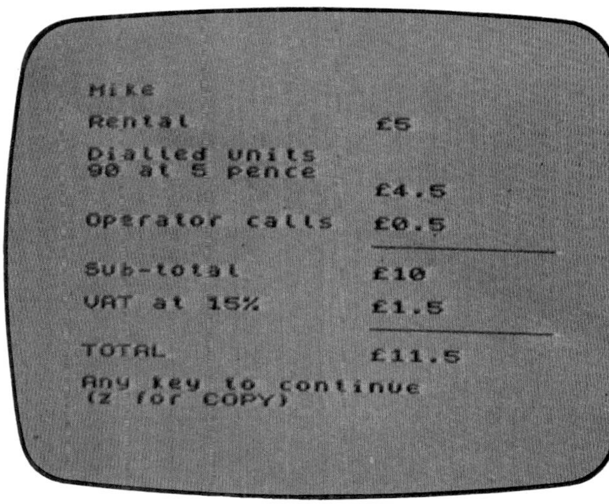

possibly put down here—even with the very small amount of BASIC you now know. A good dialect such as Applesoft BASIC contains upwards of 80 commands, usable in a wide variety of permutations. Some of the most challenging ones are those that give you access to machine code, such as PEEK, which lets you see the number stored at a certain memory address, and POKE, which lets you place a number directly into such an address; USR lets you run a whole machine-code sequence. But even if I had the room, this isn't the place for you to find out about such things. I leave you now in the capable hands (?) of your own computer, because there is no better place to learn about programming. There should be at least a short BASIC course in the manual supplied with it—though remember, this is not quite the same thing as a programming course. You need to know not only what commands to use, but also how. The manual may be inadequate, but don't despair; as soon as a new computer appears on the market, so do a rash of books about programming it. Some of these are just rip-offs, but many are excellent; the Atari range, for example, has inspired some fascinating tomes—unfortunately some very expensive ones, too. Sinclair material is cheaper, as you would expect, but some of it leaves a lot to be desired.

The best way of all to learn BASIC, though, is with a teacher. There are a number of courses organised by adult education and similar organisations, and it is worth looking around for some of these in your area. They are generally very cheap. Less formal instruction can be found at computer clubs, or from clued-up friends—though beware the enthusiast whose knowledge becomes a crutch for his ego and a club for yours! But in my opinion the best teacher of all is your own machine.

# 7. Where do I go from here?

Anywhere you can find out more about home computers, and your chosen one in particular. If you were able to contact another user or a users' group before buying, keep up the contact; have somewhere you can go to get help, advice, reassurance or dire warnings, and to share discoveries and developments you yourself have made. Even the smallest home computer isn't a finite thing; they're always full of surprises, some good and some not so good. But because of that you can rely on them not to bore you—**if** you don't let them. So, finding a users' group or computer club becomes more of a priority, even, when you've actually bought your machine. It shouldn't be

impossibly difficult; I myself know of about 70 in Britain, with another 20 or so international groups in Europe, and there are certainly more. Their addresses and officials change quite frequently, however, so listings in the monthly magazines—especially **Personal Computer World**—will be better than this or any other book can provide. If you have difficulties, though, try writing to a magazine, or to ACC (formerly the Amateur Computer Club), a national organization of computer clubs. The current address is:
Rupert Steele, Esq.
ACC Membership Secretary
St. John's College
Oxford OX1 3JP
Send a stamped self-addressed envelope.

## Computertown UK

Another useful source of information, especially if you want to compare popular models, is the **Computertown UK** scheme, a kind of amateur public-relations drive for home computers which organises open days in libraries, church halls and similar local centres; members bravely lend their own machines for you to try out, and stand by with help and guidance. Again, since the list of CTUK organizers is growing all the time, the best place to find them is through the magazines. CTUK has no commercial links, so the only bias you will find is that of owners for their own machines (which is often quite enough!).

## Magazines

In fact, as I said at the beginning, magazines are the best possible way of following this fast-changing field—once you have some idea, at least, of what they're talking about. But there are far too many of them on the shelves—about a dozen, not counting pure business publications, at the time of writing—and not all of them are good. Too many of them suffer from split personalities, trying to hook both businessman, semi-professional, hobbyist and home user, and so not catering adequately for any of them; generally the home user comes off worst, and is all too often treated with unveiled contempt. Even the best magazines fall into that trap sometimes. Since people's needs and tastes vary so widely I hesitate to recommend any particular magazine, but probably the best ones for the newcomer are **Your Computer** (with **Personal Computing Today** hard on its heels) and the huge and glossy **Personal Computer World**, probably the market leader. It gives the impression of being created by and for computer professionals, but with a sympathetic eye on newcomers. Its reviews are excellent as a rule, not skimping on the technical data but remaining literate and readable; its articles range from the chatty to the terrifyingly technical, with no concessions at all, but from the magazine as a whole you can learn a tremendous amount. And it usually carries an excellent section of club news, CTUK contacts and so on. Beyond these, specific user magazines for your particular make are always interesting, and sometimes invaluable; some of these may be American, though, and information they contain should be treated with care. If the machine is popular in Britain, there may be a British alternative or supplement. Otherwise American magazines such as **Byte** (the size of a small phone directory every month) should be avoided until you know a little more about the subject.

Magazines will also direct you to the various computer shows held around the country. In fact, they often organise them; **Personal Computer World's** annual show, held in early September in London, is usually the biggest and best for home users, but Manchester's Northern Computer Fair and the **Which Computer** show at the National Exhibition Centre, Birmingham, also have much of interest. There are many smaller shows and fairs—even some dedicated to Sinclair-related products—all over the country; follow the computer press to find the nearest. Be warned, though; many computer exhibitions are of business interest only; some of them bar under-18s (tough, but the result of bitter experience); and all of them make you pay. Check up before you set out, or you may be disappointed. In any case you will probably have to queue at the door for some time, and then fight your way through milling herds of people at all the really interesting stands. You can expect to see new products here, and perhaps even buy them at discount, but don't expect to get the kind of leisurely demonstration a good dealer will give you. And beware of impulse buying at all times.

## Books

Another way to expand your knowledge of computers is through books. Computer manuals being what they are, there are usually several books available for most popular makes of home computers, all aiming to help you squeeze the last ounce of performance out of it. There are far too many to review or list here—for Sinclair products alone there are literally dozens—but the titles below are among the best-established. There is relatively little available as yet for the newer machines in our survey; it pays to be wary of the first ones to appear, because they have generally been rushed out to cash in on the new readership. They tend to promise a lot and deliver rather less. Knowledge of a machine comes only through real experience. Also included are a few more general titles, and in particular some which look at the wider implications of the microchip in everyday life. These will both interest and disturb you, as they should; even if you discount half of what they say, the picture of the future they paint for us remains strange and revolutionary—not in any political sense, although political implications are there by the dozen. The home computer is only a small part of the dramatic developments to come—but it is one of the most crucial ones. In choosing and using your first home computer, you are taking a small step which is as much a 'giant leap' as Neil Armstrong's, and quite possibly a lot more significant. You are beginning to adapt, as quickly and painlessly as possible, to the changes that are coming; in effect, you are evolving—even if you only want to play Invaders or get your tax right for once. Small things in themselves, but they add up; they are your first bite at a very rich cake indeed. But don't just stop here—have some more...

### Origins of computers

Hawkins, Gerald S., **Stonehenge Decoded** (Fontana)
Randall, Brian, **The Origins of Digital Computing** (Springer Verlag)

### Computers in general

Evans, Dr. Christopher, **The Mighty Micro** (Gollancz)
Evans, Dr. Christopher, **The Making of the Micro** (Gollancz/Coronet)
Kidder, Tracy, **The Soul of a New Machine** (Allen Lane). American 'literary documentary' account of the development of a new microprocessor. To be filmed, apparently.
Bradbeer, Robin; de Bono, Peter; Laurie, Peter; **The Computer Book** (BBC Publications)

### Basic Programming

Albrecht, Finkel & Brown, **BASIC for Home Computers** (John Wiley & Sons Ltd.)
Alcock, Donald, **Illustrating BASIC** (Cambridge University Press). Small book, written and drawn entirely by hand; charming and accessible.
Cope, Tonia, **Computing using BASIC: An Interactive Approach** (Ellis H. Horwood/John Wiley & Sons). Good but expensive general textbook, using Research Machines BASIC.
Gosling, Peter, **Program your Microcomputer in BASIC** (Macmillan). Good, cheap book using Microsoft BASIC.
Knecht, Ken, **Microsoft BASIC** (dilithium Press). American heavyweight book, the definitive text on Microsoft BASIC.
Prigmore, Chris, **30-Hour Basic** (National Extension College/BBC). A good course intended for the BBC machine, but usable with most others; a special version for Sinclair models is available.

## Magazines

**Personal Computer World** (Computing Publications Ltd., London)
**Your Computer** (IPC Business Press Ltd., Sutton, Surrey)
**Personal Computing Today** (Argus Specialist Publications Ltd., London)
**Which Micro? & Software Review** (EMAP Business & Computer Publications Ltd., London)

**Practical Computing** (IPC Business Press Ltd., London)
**Computing Today** (Argus Specialist Publications Ltd., London)
**Micro Update** (Argus Specialist Publications Ltd., London)
**Popular Computing Weekly** (Sunshine Publications Ltd., London)
**Sinclair User** (ECC Publications Ltd., London)
**Acorn User** for Acorn and BBC micros (Addison-Wesley Publications Ltd., London)

This is just a selection of the magazines available, including the ones I feel will be most interesting and helpful to the home reader. You will find many more on the shelves of any large newsagent, but many will be heavily or wholly business-oriented.

# 8. What did that mean?

This is a short glossary of computer jargon, covering some of the commoner terms, especially those not already explained in the text. For others, try the index.

**Access:** to get information into or out of some part of the computer system.
**Accumulator (ACC):** location in the ALU where numbers for calculation are stored.
**Acronym:** name formed from initial letters of a fuller name. Jargon thrives on them.
**Algorithm:** series of logical steps to solve a problem; in other words, the core of a program. High snob value in jargon.
**Analogue:** used of information represented by some physical amount—e.g. movement of a lever, or an electrical voltage—rather than by numbers (compare **digital**).
**Array:** programming term for information laid out as if in a table or numbered list.
**Assign:** to give something, e.g. a variable, a value.
**Backup:** provisions in case something goes wrong, such as spare copies of software, or hardware service arrangements.
**Baud rate**, or **information-transfer rate:** speed, usually in bits per second, at which information passes between parts of the computer system (e.g. cassette loading of programs). Think of it as the rate at which peas pass down a pea-shooter.
**Benchmark:** fixed standard of performance against which something is measured, most often a computer's operating speed. Reviewer's joy.
**Boolean algebra:** algebraic system that deals in logical relationships and values—whether something is true or false—rather than arithmetical ones.
**Buffer:** temporary storage area for information passing from faster to slower device.
**Bug:** flaw that has somehow crept into your brilliant program. See **debugging.**
**Call:** transfer control of some operation to some part of the computer system or of the program, such as a **subroutine**.
**Character:** symbol used to represent information—numbers, letters, punctuation, Space Invader, etc. Usually equivalent to one byte.
**Character set:** limited number of symbols which computer or peripheral will recognise.
**Command:** instruction the computer will obey.
**Compatibility:** the ability of one piece of a system—hardware or software—to work with another. Commonly, the ability of software for one machine to run on another model or make.
**Corrupt:** to spoil information held in the system, or what it is held in (e.g. disks).
**Crash:** (of a program) when it stops and cannot be restarted from that point; (of a system) when it fails or ceases to operate as a system.
**Cursor:** screen **character** indicating the point at which the computer will place the next piece of information.
**Data:** any information that isn't an order to the computer.
**Debugging:** process of finding and picking the **bugs** out of your brilliant program.
**Dedicate:** to give something an exclusive use.
**Digital:** information represented by numbers (as opposed to **analogue**).

**Dump:** to shift information, usually into some safer area of the system.
**Editor:** usually, routine in operating system that lets you alter information already entered (especially earlier lines in a program).
**Error message:** signal flashed up on the screen when the computer detects a mistake in the program. May be a clear message, or a code you have to look up.
**Execute:** to do something in a program.
**File:** organised body of information, treated as a single unit by the system.
**Firmware:** software held in ROM (midway between hardware and software).
**Flowchart:** diagram showing the steps, choices and alternatives in solving a problem.
**Garbage:** information that doesn't make sense. 'Garbage in = garbage out!'
**Graphics:** anything on the screen, but consisting of pictorial rather than alphanumeric characters.
**Handshaking:** satisfactory interchange of information between different parts of the system.
**Hard copy:** information the system outputs on paper, via printer or plotter.
**Input/output (I/O):** anything through which the computer both receives and transmits information.
**Interactive:** something in or through which you and your computer respond to each other.
**Interface** (as a verb, in addition to hardware name): to connect up parts of the system compatibly.
**Jump:** instruction in program which tells the computer to go to another part of the program, usually determined by the result of a calculation.
**K:** abbreviation for **kilobyte**, which ought to mean a thousand bytes. In fact it is used to indicate 1024 bytes, $2^{10}$, a more convenient figure for a computer. (Salaries are sometimes quoted as, e.g., £10K. If they offer you that, hold them to it!)
**LCD:** Liquid Crystal Diode, method used to provide limited display (like digital watch or calculator) on some portable computers. Has been adapted for TV use, so LCD monitors may appear.
**LED:** Light-Emitting Diode, often used for on/off lights.
**Logic:** (in computer terms) systematic relationships between events expressed in mathematical form.
**Memory map:** diagram representing the 'pigeonhole' structure of a computer's total memory as if it were a single unit, instead of a series of chips, and showing how information is held in its various addresses.
**Menu:** section of a sophisticated program which shows you a list of its various functions (perhaps with information about them) and asks you to choose.
**Monitor:** (1) specialised display screen; **OR** (2) the part of the operating system which directs the input of information.
**Motherboard:** circuit board allowing supplementary circuit boards, providing extra memory and functions, to be attached.
**Network:** system of interconnected microcomputers, either local or at a distance, often sharing peripherals.
**Nibble:** would you believe half a byte? I'm afraid so—1 nibble = 4 bits.
**Octal:** numbering system based on 8; used like Hex, but largely superseded by it.
**On-line:** connected to or controlled by the CPU. A classic bit of jargon.
**Overwrite:** putting new information into some part of the system, and so erasing what was already there.
**Package:** block of software sold for a particular purpose.
**PCB** (Printed Circuit Board): circuit base with connectors etched out of fine metal film instead of wires.
**Pixel** (from **pic**ture **el**ement): the smallest available element of which a TV picture is made up.
**Port:** connector (usually some kind of plug socket) by which something can be linked to the computer's bus system.
**Portable:** used of software that can be transferred from one type or make of computer to another.
**Printout:** printed output from the system.
**Real time:** processing of information more or less instantly, generally for **interactive** uses.
**Register:** temporary memory location in microprocessor where information is stored during operations.
**Reserved word:** term or group of symbols that have a specific meaning (such as a BASIC command like RUN) to the computer, and so cannot be used as variable names in a program.
**Robot:** (coined by playwright Karel Čapek from Czech **robota**, forced labour) a computer-controlled device with sensory equipment which allows it to make decisions based on external conditions—for example, moving mechanical arms to assemble components of cars or other machinery, even other robots. Science-fiction's 'mechanical men' are one type of robot, known as an 'android'.
**Routine:** a sequence of instructions for a specific purpose; usually a program or part of one.
**Scanning:** rapid review of information by the computer.
**Source program:** program written in anything other than machine code and requiring translation. What it is written in is known as the **source language.**
**Statement:** a kind of command in a computer language.
**String:** a group of characters the computer can work with.
**Structured programming:** rigidly logical programming technique much favoured by the academic computer experts, in which the program must follow the structure of the original idea as closely as possible. A good idea, but it can make things needlessly difficult for beginners, and is a happy hunting-ground for pseuds. Half the amateurs who spout about it wouldn't know a structured program if it bit them in the leg.
**Subroutine:** 'semi-detached' and self-contained part

of a program, kept that way so it can be used several times from different parts of the program. In BASIC, subroutines are usually tacked on at the end of the program, approached by a GOSUB command with the appropriate line number; when the subroutine is completed a RETURN command directs the computer back to the next line after the GOSUB.

**Syntax:** the 'grammar' governing the way programming commands are put together. If you use them wrongly the computer will return a syntax **error message.**

**Teletext:** pages of information in a standardised format, broadcast from a database either in the marginal lines of a television picture and decoded (like the BBC's CEEFAX or ITV's ORACLE) or along phone lines (like PRESTEL). Either method can be used to send out 'telesoftware', which can be 'downloaded' directly into a computer's memory.

**Terminal:** peripheral containing keyboard and VDU, separate from main computer.

**Timesharing:** system allowing a number of users to use the operating time of a large computer simultaneously, from separate **terminals.**

**Utility:** program or routine to help you write programs or run system.

**Vapourware:** interesting new term to cover any product announced in blaze of publicity which does not yet exist in saleable form. You will become grimly familiar with it, as we did in putting this book together (cf. **Hot Air, Thin Air**).

**Variable:** symbol in a program which acts as a 'container' for information; the information can be changed, but not the name of the variable. Where a change is needed the information must be transferred to another variable.

**VDU** (Visual Display Unit): a screen on which the computer displays information. Usually a TV-type cathode-ray screen, but other, less bulky methods are being developed.

**Word:** highly inconvenient borrowing of the term to describe the standard unit of information a computer handles; in home computers, as we have seen, this is 8 bits or 1 byte, as a rule. On a 16-bit microprocessor a word would be 16 bits. This is one of the most subtly idiotic pieces of jargon, as you so often have to think twice about the context to see which meaning is being used—as with 'a 16-bit word processor', for example. Fortunately it isn't much used on home-computer territory; keep it that way.

# Index

This index was compiled and alphabetised with the aid of a specially-written program on the Sinclair Spectrum.